The Wrestling Drill Book

Second Edition

Bill Welker, EdD

Editor

Human Kinetics

Library of Congress Cataloging-in-Publication Data

The wrestling drill book / Bill Welker, editor. -- 2nd ed.
   p. cm.
1. Wrestling--Training. I. Welker, Bill, 1947-
GV1196.4.T7W74 2012
796.812--dc23

                           2012036424

ISBN: 978-1-4504-3216-0 (print)

The web addresses cited in this text were current as of October 2012, unless otherwise noted.

Developmental Editor: Anne Hall; **Assistant Editor:** Tyler M. Wolpert; **Copyeditor:** Mary Rivers; **Permissions Manager:** Martha Gullo; **Graphic Designer:** Joe Buck; **Graphic Artist:** Tara Welsch; **Cover Designer:** Keith Blomberg; **Photographs (interior):** © Human Kinetics, unless otherwise noted; **Photo Asset Manager:** Laura Fitch; **Visual Production Assistant:** Joyce Brumfield; **Photo Production Manager:** Jason Allen; **Printer:** Total Printing Systems

We thank Oak Glen High School in New Cumberland, West Virginia, for assistance in providing the location for the photo shoot for this book.

Human Kinetics books are available at special discounts for bulk purchase. Special editions or book excerpts can also be created to specification. For details, contact the Special Sales Manager at Human Kinetics.

Printed in the United States of America   10 9 8 7 6 5

The paper in this book is certified under a sustainable forestry program.

Human Kinetics
P.O. Box 5076
Champaign, IL 61825-5076
Website: www.HumanKinetics.com

In the United States, email info@hkusa.com or call 800-747-4457.
In Canada, email info@hkcanada.com.
In the United Kingdom/Europe, email hk@hkeurope.com.

For information about Human Kinetics' coverage in other areas of the world, please visit our website: **www.HumanKinetics.com**

Tell us what you think!
Human Kinetics would love to hear what we can do to improve the customer experience. Use this QR code to take our brief survey.

E5781

This book is dedicated to the late coach Mal Paul and the late coach Lyman "Beans" Weaver of Shamokin High School in Pennsylvania. These men knew the significance of drill work for producing championship teams and wrestlers. As mat mentors, they not only developed winning athletes but also molded boys into men, epitomizing integrity, hard work, and perseverance. Coach Paul and coach Weaver have since been inducted into the Pennsylvania chapter of the National Wrestling Hall of Fame.

Mal Paul
Head wrestling coach
Shamokin High School
1946–1965

Lyman "Beans" Weaver
Assistant wrestling coach
Shamokin High School
1950–1965

Contents

Drill Finder

Key

Drill level of difficulty: ⊝ = Novice;   ⊝⊝ = Intermediate;   ⊝⊝⊝ = Advanced

Drill category: Ⓢ = Solitary; Ⓟ = Partner

Key

Drill level of difficulty: ⊝ = Novice; ⊝⊝ = Intermediate; ⊝⊝⊝ = Advanced

Drill category: Ⓢ = Solitary; Ⓟ = Partner

Key

Drill level of difficulty: ⊖ = Novice; ⊖⊖ = Intermediate; ⊖⊖⊖ = Advanced

Drill category: Ⓢ = Solitary; Ⓟ = Partner

Foreword

I have the privilege to endorse the second edition of *The Wrestling Drill Book*. Dr. Bill Welker, editor, has created another edition of the volume that is even better in quality and quantity. Not only does it include the addition of many new wrestling and training drills, but it also incorporates two new chapters dealing with footwork and upper-body throws.

The chapter authors are successful high school and collegiate coaches from across the United States. These coaches have 400 years of combined experience in their areas of expertise. They develop their chapters in a step-by-step format that leads coaches and wrestlers from basic to complex drills. In fact, coaches and wrestlers are exposed to a variety of maneuvers and countermaneuvers throughout the entire book.

The Wrestling Drill Book allows coaches of all levels (youth to international wrestling) to select the maneuvers that are suited to their wrestlers' individual abilities.

The book concludes with a chapter that provides coaches with preseason and in-season practice strategies that revolve around the drills emphasized in the book. It includes motivational coaching and evaluation techniques to keep the wrestlers focused on their goals throughout the season. Some great off-season activities will keep the wrestlers actively conditioning themselves for wrestling throughout the entire year.

The second edition of *The Wrestling Drill Book* is a great reference devoted to producing successful wrestlers and championship wrestling programs. They say sequels are rarely as good as the originals. Such is not the case with the second edition of *The Wrestling Drill Book*. You were smart in adding this book to your library!

Zeke Jones
Head coach of the 2012 U.S. Olympic freestyle wrestling team
World champion
Olympic silver medalist

Acknowledgments

I would like to thank every one of the coaching contributors who made *The Wrestling Drill Book* a best-seller. Their efforts on the first and second editions are greatly appreciated.

Thanks to Mike Dyer, strength and conditioning coach at Rocky Mountain High School in Colorado, who shared his expertise in the development of chapter 8, Conditioning. He provided terrific insight on the philosophy and technique of weightlifting. Mike also provided input regarding the athlete's core strength exercises. His ideas on wrestling-specific variations of lifting and conditioning were instrumental in the development of the chapter.

A special note of appreciation goes to the demonstrators—Ronnell Green, Joel Timmons, Abby Rush, Cody Miller, Ronnie Green, Bryce Rush, Eric Banks, Jonny Davis, Tyler Brown, Josh Cornell, Josh Sokolowski, Nathan Kirk, Matt Shurina, Geremy Paige, and Doug Eddy—for their dedicated efforts during the photo and video sessions. Also, thanks to coach Larry Shaw and the administration at Oak Glen High School in New Cumberland, West Virginia, for the use of their mat room. We appreciate the expertise of coach Shaw as well as that of Coach Buzz Evans of Wheeling Park High School in Wheeling, West Virginia. Kudos to Ray Marling and Chris Diserio for their officiating expertise in the photo and video phase of the book. A special thanks to Wayne Hicks for his glowing tribute to the late coach Ed Peery, whose contributions to wrestling are nonpareil.

Thanks to Andrew R. Welker for his technological support. Likewise, appreciation goes to photographer Mark Anderman and videographer Gregg Henness for their undaunted patience. A special thank-you to my friends, the late coach Joseph J. Thomas and the late Sgt. Mark J. Gerrity, USMC, men who cherished every aspect of the sport of wrestling.

I also want to thank Human Kinetics staff members Jason Muzinic, Ted Miller, Holly Gilly, Anne Hall, Tyler Wolpert, Tina Kinder, Jennifer Mulcahey, Amanda Bryan, Bill Johnson, Keith Blomberg, Sue Outlaw, and Mary Rivers for their professionalism throughout the development of this book. They believed in my dream to produce a drill book of utmost benefit to wrestling enthusiasts at all levels of the sport.

A loving thank-you to my wife, Peggy, for her words of encouragement and patience from the beginning to the conclusion of this writing project. And finally, an endearing memorial thanks to our parents, William and Dorothy Welker and Howard and Margaret Bainbridge, who taught Peggy and me to believe in ourselves and to thank God for all his blessings.

Dr. William A. "Bill" Welker
Editor

Introduction

A fact of life in wrestling has been and will always remain the same: Champions are made in the practice room. The prime ingredient is *drill, drill, drill* during all wrestling workout sessions. This creates something akin to that elusive realm known as athletic perfection.

Without move perfection in wrestling, the wrestler who must think before reacting is lost. One high school coach put it bluntly: "If I have to yell at you what to do during a match, it's probably too late. That's why the hell we drill."

The bottom line is that wrestlers must have the desire to be number one. And that desire to be the best can be fulfilled only with a willingness to drill until a move becomes second nature, regardless of the phase of wrestling. Dr. Welker believes so strongly in the significance of drill work that he has composed the following success-oriented equation:

The 3 Ds = The 3 Ms

Dynamic **d**rill **d**evelopment = **m**aximum **m**uscle **m**emory

In essence, never underestimate the importance of drill work. Wrestlers often find drill work as the most boring aspect of wrestling. That is why, as the coach, you must constantly stress to your wrestlers the critical nature of drill work during every practice session.

This book presents wrestling drills that have proven advantageous via the test of time. They are founded on the essentials of the mat sport. The contributors of this book were determined to create a wrestling resource that would assist coaches at all levels in producing championship-caliber wrestlers.

The drills are based on the importance of proper hip positioning (or center of gravity) in all facets of wrestling, a fundamental aspect of the mat sport often overlooked by coaches. The drills are presented in a manner that leads the participants to the big picture of actual wrestling.

Chapter 1 concentrates on essential movement drills in the areas of takedowns, escapes and reversals, and riding and pinning combinations. It includes the corresponding counter drills for the various initial drills demonstrated. Coach Bill Archer, takes you step by step through each drill.

In chapter 2, a new addition to this book, Dr. Bill Welker and coach Larry Shaw discuss footwork by stressing agility, quickness, and balance. This chapter focuses on an area only modestly dealt with in other wrestling texts. It includes drills to improve wrestlers' maneuvering on their feet. As we all realize, the wrestler who is better on his feet has the upper hand in any given match.

Chapter 3 addresses the all-important takedown. Coach Dave LaMotte guides you through various takedown situations. He also explains how to counter takedown attacks.

Chapter 4, also new for this second edition, covers advanced throws and takedown drills. Coach Larry Shaw and Dr. Bill Welker offer coaches a repertoire of upper-body moves, including the rarely discussed pancake takedown series, which can be performed by wrestlers of all shapes and sizes.

Collegiate coach Pat Pecora focuses on escapes and reversals in chapter 5. He also describes numerous counters to escape and reversal situations.

Chapter 6 centers on rides and pinning combination drills. The late coach Ed Peery and current coach of the Naval Academy Bruce Burnett share their vast knowledge regarding this area of wrestling. Experts in their field, Peery and Burnett develop the proper transition from rides to their complementary pinning combinations. Furthermore, they illustrate many countermaneuvers to various rides and pinning positions.

The emphasis in chapter 7 is on advanced pinning combination drills. Coach Jim Akerly and West Virginia University head coach Craig Turnbull give vivid descriptions of prepinning drills as well as advanced drills for pinning situations.

Chapter 8 presents a myriad of conditioning drills. This includes drills for strength, endurance, agility, flexibility, and cardiorespiratory enhancement. The purpose of these drills is twofold. First, the drills assist in developing wrestler conditioning. Second, they prepare wrestlers for live-action wrestling. Coach Ken Taylor, assisted by strength coach Mike Dyer, does an outstanding job emphasizing the importance of these conditioning drills to producing championship wrestlers.

Dr. Bill Welker's final chapter brings it all together. Chapter 9 demonstrates how to incorporate the many drills in this book into your daily workout sessions. It also presents a year-round road map that leads you from preseason practices to off-season activities. New additions to the chapters include group work during workout sessions, practice wrestle-offs (or eliminations), practice and wrestler evaluations, and models of preseason and in-season activities and practices.

The drills emphasized in this book have been developed and used for decades by highly successful coaches throughout the United States. They work because they are grounded on sound principles of wrestling.

As a responsible and dedicated coach, you know the level of knowledge and ability of the wrestlers under your charge. The format of this book allows you to choose those drills that would be most beneficial for your competitors.

Proper drill instruction breeds champions and winning teams in all sports at every level of competition. *The Wrestling Drill Book, Second Edition*, offers a drill-oriented approach to wrestling and will guide you in the right direction.

Essential Movements

Bill Archer

" *The way to avoid roadblocks to learning is to ask questions.* "

Joseph J. Thomas

Wrestling, like most sports, is a competition made up of movements and involves the starting and stopping of motion. During the infancy of wrestling in America, coaches taught holds; today, coaches teach *moves*, or *essential movements*.

Essential movements in wrestling need to be drilled correctly and repeatedly in order for the wrestler to have success during competition. Thus the structure of drills must be such that the essential skills develop the ability to execute moves naturally.

The coaches' and wrestlers' attitudes toward the drilling process are of paramount importance. Letting wrestlers go slowly and thoughtlessly through the motions makes the drills lose much of their value. The coaches and wrestlers must perform drill work as closely to live wrestling as possible.

The following movement drills prepare wrestlers for those drills that promote perfection of techniques in all areas of wrestling. With the completion of movement drills, the wrestlers have a deeper understanding of proper movement when practicing drills in all facets of the sport. Introduce these movement drills at the beginning of the wrestling season. In the following movement drills, and the drills throughout the rest of the book, wrestler 1 and wrestler 2 will be referred to as W1 and W2.

MOVEMENT DRILLS
IN NEUTRAL POSITION

There is no area in wrestling more important than the neutral position; matches are often won or lost in this area. Coaches need to place major emphasis on movement drills in the neutral position. If a wrestler is weak on his feet, he will be at a disadvantage during the rigors of competition.

Stance

An essential wrestling stance must be both offensive and defensive in nature. In this position, a wrestler can quickly adjust to changing situations and is prepared to attack or to defend his opponent's attack.

Emphasize the following fundamentals of stance and movement:

1. Beware of extreme positions. For example, always attempt to keep the feet no more than shoulder-width apart for sound balance. Also, position elbows in front of the body, slightly bent toward each other. This prevents opponents from gaining inside control.
2. Keep compact with a low center of gravity.
3. Never cross your feet.
4. Tuck your head, facing the opponent's midsection.
5. Keep elbows against the body and palms facing each other.
6. Take small steps, except when attacking.

The following drills prepare the wrestlers to hone skills related to a solid and defensive stance.

CHANGING LEVEL FOR PENETRATION

Setup

W2 stands with his legs well enough apart so W1 can penetrate through them (*a*). W1 is facing W2 in the neutral stance previously described.

Action

W1 lowers his hips and steps forward toward W2. Next, W1 penetrates through W2's legs, scooting on his hands and knees underneath W2's body (*b*). W1 completes the drill by returning to his original stance facing away from W2 (*c*). Have wrestlers change positions and repeat the drill, continuing to repeat this alternating sequence until, as with all drills, you are satisfied with their performance.

Coaching Points

This drill emphasizes the importance of lowering the hips (or center of gravity) before attacking an opponent's legs. It also demonstrates to the wrestlers the significance of penetrating through their opponents, especially when attempting a double-leg takedown.

HEAD-IN-CHEST PENETRATION

Setup

W2 holds W1's head on his chest in the standing position (*a*). W1 faces W2 in the basic neutral stance previously described.

Action

W1 penetrates knee-over-toe, grabbing a single leg, driving in, and picking up the leg (*b* and *c*). He then drops the leg and takes the same shot on the opposite leg.

Coaching Points

The primary purpose of this drill is for the drill wrestler to back up the drill partner with each shot. It also teaches the wrestlers about the importance of making a second effort when the initial maneuver is unsuccessful in match competition. This drill further assists wrestlers in learning to keep their heads positioned properly when performing certain single-leg takedowns.

SPRAWL-BACK

Setup

This is a solitary drill in which each wrestler starts in a square stance in the neutral position (*a*).

Action

On the whistle, the wrestler sprawls to the mat, landing on hands and feet with a slight twist of the hips (*b*).

Coaching Point

Emphasize that the knees should not touch the mat when sprawling. The wrestlers need to understand that dropping to the knees when sprawling allows their opponents the opportunity to pull their legs in for the takedown.

PUMMELING

Setup

The drill partners start from the overhook and underhook position, with the lead leg always on the underhook side. They must also have their knees slightly bent, positioning their heads on their overhook side (*a*).

Action

On the whistle, the wrestlers repeatedly attempt the underhook position by digging into their partner's armpit, alternating underhook arms during the drill (*b*). Their heads rotate to the opposite side as they switch from the overhook to the underhook. The wrestlers' feet should also be moving with their upper bodies, always keeping the lead foot on the underhook side.

Coaching Points

This drill emphasizes the importance of inside control when wrestling in the neutral position. It also assists the wrestlers in becoming more aggressive as they work to gain inside control during actual competition.

a

b

PUMMELING TO A DUCK-UNDER

Setup

The two wrestlers start from the overhook and underhook position (*a*).

Action

As each partner starts to dig in on the overhook side, W1 raises his under-hook elbow high, forcing W2's elbow above his shoulder (*b*). The move sets up W1's opportunity for the duck-under. At this point, W1 lowers his hips as he steps behind W2 with his left leg, ducking his head under W2's arm (*c*). W1 finishes the move by coming up behind W2 and locking his hands around W2's body.

Coaching Points

This drill emphasizes lowering the hips (or center of gravity) before execut-ing the duck-under takedown. Stress the importance of staying tight against an opponent's body when executing the duck-under. Also, stress the need to arch the head back so an opponent cannot reestablish his original arm position, blocking the duck-under maneuver.

11

6

DRILL

SPIN

Setup

W2 stabilizes his position on his knees and elbows, palms facing each other. W1, who will perform the spin drill, puts his chest on top of W2's back (*a*).

Action

On the whistle, W1 begins his spin, blocking W2's triceps with his near arm in the direction he is spinning (*b*). As he turns the corner, W1 takes short choppy steps. He continues spinning in the same direction until the coach blows the whistle for him to change direction (*c*).

Coaching Point

For full mobility, the drill wrestler needs to stay off his knees throughout the drill.

MOVEMENT DRILLS
IN DEFENSIVE POSITION

Proper defensive position has been neglected in recent years; coaches should spend more time teaching it. The wrestler with insufficient defensive positioning skills is an easier target for tilting or pinning.

7

DRILL

STAND-UP ON THE WALL

Setup

The wrestlers put themselves in the defensive referee's position with the side of their body against the wrestling room wall (*a*).

Action

They then quickly stand up, stepping with their outside leg and placing their back against the wall. Their upper legs should be parallel to the mat (*b*).

Coaching Point

This drill promotes stand-up quickness and proper positioning after the stand-up.

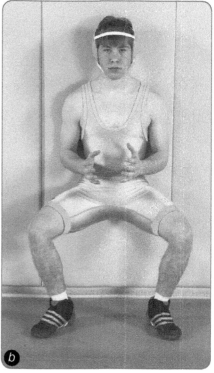

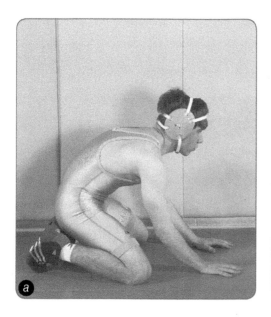

HOLDING YOUR BASE

Setup

W1 and W2 are in the referee's position (*a*).

Action

On the whistle, W1 must avoid being forced down to the mat. During the drill, W1 spreads his base and goes to both his elbows and hands, while W2 attempts to drive him off his base (*b*).

Coaching Point

Stress to the wrestlers that they must not drop to the belly because that is when opponents can turn them onto their backs.

STAND-UP AGAINST A SPIRAL RIDE

Setup

In this drill, W2 starts in the spiral ride position, with his right hand locked inside W1's far leg and his left arm across W1's upper chest. W1 is in the basic defensive referee's position (*a*).

Action

On the whistle, W1 scoots his inside knee away and pushes his back against W2's chest. W1 then raises his outside leg to place his foot on the mat. At the same time, W1 isolates W2's inside hand with both his hands (*b*). W1 extends W2's inside hand away from his body while driving off his front foot to a standing position to set up his escape (*c*).

Coaching Points

Emphasize the significance of quickness and hand control when standing up. Stress that the defensive wrestler keep his back perpendicular to the mat prior to standing up.

FINISHING THE STAND-UP, CUT-AWAY

Setup

W2 assumes the defensive referee's position. W1 then leans his back against W2's side in a crouching position (*a*).

Action

On the coach's signal, W1 raises his right arm and leg to set up his cut-away (*b*). Finally, W1 turns to his left and pushes away, facing W2 (*c*). The drill is repeated, using the left arm and leg before the wrestlers reverse drill positions.

Coaching Point

Stress the importance of the quick push-away when securing the escape maneuver.

SWITCH-RESWITCH

Setup

W1 starts on the bottom in the referee's position. W2 is in the conventional offensive referee's position.

Action

W1 starts the drill by crossing his inside hand over the outside hand (*a*). He then sits through and reaches back for the inside of W2's near leg. At this point, W2 keeps his hand inside W1's leg (*b*). While W1 comes around and behind, W2 reswitches (*c* and *d*).

Coaching Points

The drill should last approximately 10 to 15 seconds. Emphasize leg control for both wrestlers when switching and reswitching. Note: Beginners have a tendency to reach over their opponents' backs when switching.

UPPER-SHOULDER ROLL

Setup

This is a solitary drill in which each wrestler starts with his head and knees on the mat and hands on his hips.

Action

In this position, each wrestler rolls one direction on his upper shoulders and elbows, pushing off his toes (*a*), and then changes direction on the sound of the whistle (*b*). This solitary drill can last 15 to 30 seconds.

Coaching Points

The purpose of this drill is to teach the wrestlers to roll on the top of their shoulders rather than the middle of the back, a bad habit that must be stopped. The drill also prepares wrestlers for the Granby-Roll series.

MOVEMENT DRILLS
IN OFFENSIVE POSITION

The primary goal in the offensive position is to score a fall. This cannot be accomplished if a wrestler is weak in the ability to ride his opponent. Movement drills in the offensive position can aid the wrestler in perfecting riding and pinning skills.

SCRAMBLING

Setup

The coach places W1 in any unusual position pressing against W2 and facing away from W2.

Action

On the whistle, W2 can move in any direction. It is the responsibility of W1 to quickly adjust his body to be in proper riding position. In doing so, W1 should first attack W2's lower-back area prior to securing a proper ride of his choosing.

Coaching Point

This drill prepares the offensive wrestler to react to the unexpected at any time during the match. You can vary the drill by telling the offensive wrestler he cannot grab the ankle, ride the legs, or use a tight waist. This is a unique approach to entice the offensive wrestler to initiate alternative breakdowns.

FOLLOWING THE HIPS

Setup

W2 is in the bottom referee's position with W1 on top on his feet behind W2 and his hands on W2's hips.

Action

On the whistle, W2 continuously sits out and turns in or moves forward. W1's responsibility is to keep a firm hold on the hips while maneuvering on his feet and staying behind W2.

Coaching Point

The purpose of this drill is to teach the wrestlers to ride behind an opponent by not riding too high, staying on the opponent's hips.

Variation

A variation of this drill is to have the offensive wrestler place his chest on the defensive wrestler's lower back with his hands on the defensive wrestler's hips. They then perform the same drill movements. The offensive wrestler's goal is to keep his chest on the defensive wrestler's lower back.

LIFT AND RETURN

Setup

The wrestlers are standing, with W1 in control behind W2 with his hands locked together in the clap position, left hand over right hand (*a*).

Action

W1 steps to the side, bending his knees to a squat position (*b*). Next, W1 lifts W2 off the mat, bringing his right knee up (*c*). This turns W2 parallel to the mat. As W2 is returned to the mat, landing on his side, W1 simultaneously drops to both knees and unlocks his hands.

Coaching Point

This breakdown drill teaches wrestlers to correctly and safely return the opponent to the mat from the standing position.

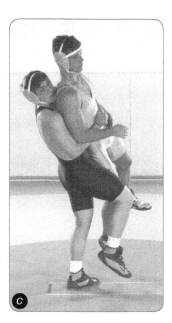

SPIRAL RIDE TO NAVY EXPOSURE

Setup

The wrestlers start in the spiral ride position (*a*).

Action

W1, rotating counterclockwise, pulls W2 to his near hip and quickly slides his right arm over W2's top leg and under W2's bottom leg. W1 also has his right arm bent with his elbow touching the mat (*b*). At this point, W2's legs are lifted by W1, who rests his elbow on his lap as he steps up (*c*). W1 completes the drill by stacking W2 on his back by driving him forward (*d*).

Coaching Points

This drill teaches the wrestlers to move from the spiral ride position to a pinning situation as quickly as possible. Also, point out the importance of the offensive wrestler keeping his head in front of the defensive wrestler when the navy is secured.

SPIRAL RIDE TO HOOK AND PIN

Setup

The wrestlers start in the spiral ride position (*a*).

Action

W1 pulls W2 to his near hip while hooking his top arm (*b*). He then starts pulling W2 to his back. W1 finishes the drill by overhooking W2's head and pressing his shoulders to the mat (*c*).

Coaching Point

This drill teaches the wrestlers to move from the spiral ride position to another pinning situation. Far too often wrestlers do not follow through with successful ride techniques and risk being warned or penalized for stalling.

CONCLUSION

Essential movements, or what some call the basics, are critical in preparing athletes to deal with the rigors of wrestling. The preceding drills are just the beginning of a journey toward developing championship wrestlers, a journey that will involve more and more drill work on the mats. As the coach, you must continue to stress to your athletes the significance of repeatedly practicing moves. Essential movement drills are necessary for perfecting all wrestling maneuvers.

Wrestling is a very complex sport. There are a number of areas that must be taught by the coach and learned by the wrestlers. Failing to do so will lead to a less-than-successful wrestling program.

Essential movement drills are stepping stones that prepare wrestlers for performing takedown, escape and reversal, riding, and pinning combination drills. Think of the essential movement drills as prerequisites to the many success-oriented drills in the remaining chapters of this book.

Chapter 2 introduces drills that will improve your wrestlers' footwork abilities. All successful wrestlers display outstanding agility, quickness, and balance skills on their feet. If you want your wrestlers to be competent takedown artists, they must first develop fundamental footwork skills.

CHAPTER

2

Footwork: Agility, Quickness, and Balance

Larry Shaw and Bill Welker

" *It is a rough road that leads to heights of greatness.* "

Seneca

Footwork is an important training aspect in many sports, and wrestling is no exception. In wrestling, it is rarely given any serious attention. This chapter offers a sampling of the many footwork drills that a coach can incorporate in a practice framework. Footwork should be stressed at the beginning of the season when conditioning is a central focus.

The components to emphasize are agility, quickness, and balance. They are the key to becoming a more successful wrestler in the neutral position.

Agility is the ability to change direction and body position while staying under control (also discussed in chapter 8). Closely associated with agility is quickness. Wrestling is more a sport of quick movement than one of speed. Quickness is the ability to move rapidly and energetically with physical dexterity. Finally, wrestling is a sport that requires superior balance tactics. Balance is the skill of retaining physical equilibrium without losing one's footing.

The following exercises will assist you in producing wrestlers who are adept in their footwork. These drills emphasize all three footwork skills: agility, quickness, and balance.

SINGLE-FOOT HOPPING

Setup

The wrestlers face the coach in the wrestling room.

Action

This balance exercise involves holding one foot behind the back while hopping on other foot, either back and forth or side to side as instructed by the coach. This drill can last 15 seconds or until the wrestler loses his balance. Repeat with the opposite foot.

Coaching Points

This solitary drill can be performed in groups or as a whole-squad activity at the beginning of practice. Stress the importance of the wrestlers keeping their balance, which is very important during competition.

19

CIRCLE SHUFFLE

Setup

The wrestlers stand on the outside boundary line facing the coach who is in the middle of the mat.

Action

Wrestlers move sideways in a circle without crossing one foot over the other. Wrestlers change direction on the whistle. This wrestling-specific agility drill teaches the wrestlers not to cross their feet in the wrestling breakdown position (*a* and *b*).

Coaching Points

Although a solitary activity, this can be a whole-team activity during the beginning of practice exercises. It is imperative that you emphasize the importance of not crossing the feet!

WRESTLING BREAKDOWN SPRINT AND JOG

Setup

Wrestlers should be in the neutral breakdown position facing the coach.

Action

On the coach's whistle, wrestlers will perform intervals of sprint and jog sequences (*a*). Then, again on the coach's command ("Hit it!"), the wrestlers drop to the mat on their elbows and toes (*b*) and spring back to their feet as quickly as possible, returning to the breakdown position. It can be implemented as a whole-squad drill during opening exercise or finishing up exercises at the end of practice.

Coaching Points

This quickness activity should last 30 seconds to a minute. Do not only stress quickness, but also that the wrestlers drop to the mat on elbows and toes without touching their knees to the mat.

STANDING BALANCE CHECK

Setup

Each wrestler grabs his partner's wrist with one hand while holding his opposite leg with his other hand.

Action

On the coach's signal, each wrestler tries to push and pull his partner off balance. This drill can last 15 seconds or until one wrestler loses his balance. Then repeat the drill with the opposite wrist and foot. This game–like partner drill–can be performed at the end of practice as an intra-squad competition.

Coaching Point

See to it that the wrestlers are aware of keeping their balance during the activity, and how it relates to good balance during competition.

CRAB WALK

Setup

This solitary agility drill starts with the wrestlers on all fours (feet and hands).

Action

On the coach's signal, the wrestlers move forward, backward, and from side to side. The activity should last approximately 30 seconds with the chest down (*a*); then repeat the action with the chest up (*b*).

Coaching Points

This drill can be initiated during the beginning of practice exercises or in groups. Stress to your wrestlers the importance of not touching any other part of their bodies to the mat but their hands and feet.

TOE SPRING

Setup

The wrestlers are in the crouched position.

Action

This is a solitary balance and agility drill. The wrestlers lock their hands behind their backs. On the coach's command, the wrestlers toe spring to the front and back and from side to side, with their feet springing as high as they can off the mat.

Coaching Points

This footwork drill can be performed during opening exercises, in groups, or as a whole-squad activity. Instruct the wrestlers to spring as high as they can during each jump.

ONE-FOOT STATIONARY BALANCE

Setup

The wrestlers stand with feet shoulder width apart, facing the coach.

Action

This balance drill is performed with arms spread out to the side. Keeping his arms spread, the wrestler stretches one leg forward as straight as possible, balancing on the other foot (*a*). In this position, the wrestler lowers his body as low as he can go (*b*) and then straightens up again. Perform the drill five times for each foot.

Coaching Points

This drill could be group work or a whole-squad activity. Tell the wrestlers that this is a difficult balance drill to perform, and not to become frustrated. Be their cheerleader.

CARIOCA

Setup

The wrestlers start by facing the coach with arms extended.

Action

The wrestlers side step their feet (front to back), first moving to the right and then to the left on the coach's signal (*a* and *b*).

Coaching Points

This traditional agility and quickness drill has been used for many decades for all sports, including wrestling. The drill could be done as a group or as a whole-squad activity. Watch the wrestlers carefully. Many have trouble performing this agility drill at first.

a

b

AIRPLANE SPRAWL

Setup

In this partner quickness drill, W1 stands straight, with arms stretched out to the side like an airplane. W2 is in the breakdown position with his head an inch away from the other wrestler's chest (*a*).

Action

On the whistle, W1 will sprawl back on his toes as W2 is attempting a double-leg takedown (*b*). The wrestlers will take turns in each position to see who is quicker.

Coaching Points

This drill should be performed in groups or as a whole-squad activity. The wrestlers must be instructed not to drop to their knees when sprawling back. That is the key factor regarding this quickness drill.

SPIN TO BREAKDOWN

Setup

The wrestler faces the coach with legs shoulder width apart.

Action

In this solitary balance drill, the wrestler spreads his arms and spins either clockwise or counterclockwise, following the coach's directions, for 10 to 15 seconds. On the coach's whistle, the wrestler abruptly stops spinning and assumes the wrestling neutral breakdown position, facing forward, without losing his balance (a-c).

Coaching Points

This drill could fit into the opening exercise phase or be done in groups. This balance drill prepares wrestlers for moments of "dizziness" when spinning around during the rigors of competition.

MOUNTAIN CLIMB

Setup

The wrestlers begin on their toes and hands with belly down, facing their coach.

Action

On the whistle, the wrestlers begin climbing their feet back and forth in place. On the second whistle, they stop.

Coaching Points

The wrestlers must be informed to face forward at the coach during the drill. This 30-second, solitary quickness drill could be done in a group or as whole-squad activity.

FORWARD AND REVERSE JUMP ROPE

Setup

The wrestlers face the coach ready to jump rope.

Action

The wrestlers jump rope on the coach's signal, going forward or reverse (backward) on the coach's command. The drill should last approximately 60 seconds and be performed as a group activity.

Coaching Points

Stress to the wrestlers how important it is to perfect their jump rope skills as they pertain to hand-foot sequence agility and quickness. Every wrestling coach should incorporate rope jumping into his conditioning program. It best fits into group work activities. Jumping rope is also discussed in chapter 8's discussion of conditioning, along with a reference to Buddy Lee's jump rope Web site.

Variations

This drill can be performed using single foot jumping. Wrestlers can also try crossing their hands while jumping rope.

SPRINT-IN-PLACE

Setup

The wrestlers face the coach in the wrestling breakdown position.

Action

On the coach's command, they sprint in place. Still sprinting in place, the wrestlers change direction when the coach directs them to turn left, right, or forward (facing the coach).

Coaching Points

The coach should randomly choose the direction in which he wants the wrestlers to turn. This quickness drill is an offshoot of footwork drills found in every football coach's practice plan. It is an effective whole-squad quickness drill that should last about one minute. The coach should explain to the wrestlers how important it is for them to sprint as quickly as possible during the activity.

HIGH STEP

Setup

The wrestlers face the coach.

Action

On the coach's instructions, the wrestlers will high step forward, backward, and side to side. It should last about one minute.

Coaching Points

This solitary agility and quickness exercise consists of high stepping like a running back or offensive end football player. The coach should randomly choose the direction in which he wants the wrestlers to move. This is an effective whole-squad quickness drill that should last about one minute. Emphasize to the wrestlers to properly high step to waist level.

ZIG-ZAG

Setup

The wrestler positions himself facing the cone and coach.

Action

The wrestler moves forward explosively and then backward, moving from left to right through a course of cones (*a-c*).

Coaching Points

The wrestlers should maintain a low athletic stance while moving through the course. Once through the course, the wrestlers can return, this time moving from right to left.

CONE SHUTTLE RUN

Setup

The wrestler faces the straight line of cones.

Action

The wrestlers weave between cones, pick up a dumbbell (10 to 20 pounds) at the far end, and return to the starting point (*a-c*).

Coaching Points

This is a great solitary drill for quickness and agility. To further motivate the wrestlers, you can time them to see who is the fastest.

Variation

If the coach is working with youth wrestlers, replace the dumbbell with a wooden block.

LATERAL DISC HOP

Setup

Set up a row of discs about 1 to 2 feet apart. The wrestler stands beside the first disc facing the coach.

Action

The wrestler begins the course beside the first disc, facing the coach. He then hops both feet across the disc (*a*), landing in the space between the first and second disc. He continues hopping to the end of the course and then returns (hopping) to the starting point.

Coaching Point

Be sure to instruct the wrestlers to hop with both feet together. One foot should not be lower than the other foot when hopping.

Variation

A variation would be hopping forward through the course (*b*).

STEP-UP

Setup

The wrestler stands facing the gym bleachers or box (*a*).

Action

The wrestlers step up on the first step with the right foot and then the left foot (*b*), and then return to the floor with the same foot sequence as many times as possible during the 30- to 45-second time period.

Coaching Point

This is a quickness activity. Stress the importance of proper foot sequence when the wrestlers perform this drill.

Variation

This activity can be performed as a group or as a whole-squad exercise.

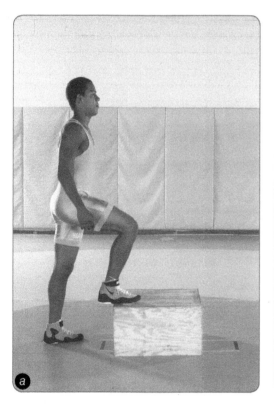

LADDER

Setup

Lay a ladder on the mat and have the wrestler stand facing it.

Action

The wrestler quickly steps between the rungs to the far side (*a*) and then returns to the starting point.

Coaching Point

This is an agility and quickness drill. The wrestlers must be made aware of the importance of performing the activity in the shortest amount of time as possible. You might time them to see who is the quickest.

Variation

This activity could be performed during group work or as a whole-squad drill. A variation is stepping laterally across the ladder (*b*).

AGILITY DOTS

Setup

Place five numbered dots in the shape of a rectangle with one dot in the center.

Action

The wrestler starts on the middle dot. When the coach calls a number, he jumps to the appropriate dot (*a*).

Coaching Points

The coach should explain the significance of the wrestlers moving as quickly as possible to the designated dot number, and not losing their balance when hopping on one foot. This plyometric activity should be done in groups.

Variation

A variation would be hopping on one foot to the appropriate dot without losing balance (*b*).

HOPPER BALANCE

Setup

W1 holds W2's right foot in front of him at waist level.

Action

On the coach's signal, W1 pushes and pulls his partner's foot, attempting to make him lose balance.

Coaching Points

Drill for 15 seconds on each foot; it should be done in groups. Safety first. Make sure there is enough room so the wrestlers don't collide into each other.

 DRILL

39

PLANK CIRCLE

Setup

Wrestlers are in the up-phase, push-up position with hands on the mat. (*a*).

Action

On the coach's signal, the wrestlers start moving on his toes around in a circle (*b*). On each whistle, the wrestlers reverse direction. The drill should last between 30 to 45 seconds.

Coaching Point

The coach must emphasize that the wrestlers keep their bodies straight or in the plank position when performing the activity.

Variation

This is an agility and quickness drill that can be performed in groups. A variation would be hop-stepping on one foot.

a

b

LUNGE

Setup

The wrestler starts in the standing position facing the coach.

Action

The wrestler lifts up his right leg to waist level or higher (*a*) and either lunges forward (*b*) or pivots laterally from side to side. Repeat with the left leg.

Coaching Points

The coach should instruct the wrestler to lift each leg as high as possible. The whole squad can do this activity at the beginning of wrestling practice.

Variation

A variation of this drill, using dumbbells, is discussed in chapter 8.

LONG JUMP

Setup

The wrestler faces the coach with legs bent ready to spring off his toes.

Action

The wrestler jumps as quickly and as far forward as possible across the length of the wrestling room (*a* and *b*). The less time the feet are on the mat the better.

Coaching Points

This is a plyometric agility and quickness drill. Explain the importance of jumping as far across the mat with as few jumps as possible. The activity can be performed as group work or as a whole-squad drill.

THE SCISSOR

Setup

The wrestler starts with one foot in front of the boundary line and the other foot behind it (*a*).

Action

At the coach's signal, the wrestler repeatedly, and as quickly as possible, switches the position of his feet (*b*). Drill for 15 seconds.

Coaching Points

The coach should instruct the wrestler to count how many scissor switches he can make during the 15-second period, and try to improve the number of times during subsequent tries. This is a quickness and agility drill that can be performed as group work or as a whole-squad drill.

Variation

A variation is hopping with both feet across the line.

CONCLUSION

As previously emphasized, footwork in wrestling has rarely been discussed in the contemporary mat sport literature. As a former wrestler who was exposed to many agility, quickness, and balance drills, I did not initially understand the significance of such drill work. It was only during real match encounters that I understood the need for footwork exercises. You, as coaches, must see to it that your squad is familiarized with footwork activities, from youth to the international level. In doing so, you are better preparing your wrestlers for the rigors of highly competitive events where agility, quickness, and balance are paramount.

Keep in mind that many of the footwork drills offered in this chapter can be introduced as games during your practices. Thus your wrestlers can enjoy such activities in practice while improving their footwork skills. It's a win-win drill approach that will be a positive addition to your entire wrestling program.

In chapter 3, you will be introduced to wrestling's number one match priority—takedowns. Every wrestler must definitely excel on his feet if he expects to succeed in the mat sport.

Takedowns

Dave LaMotte

" *Make the most of yourself, for that is all there is of you.* "

Ralph Waldo Emerson

The objective in wrestling is to score a fall. When wrestlers are aggressively pursuing the fall, the action in the match is a lot more exciting for the fans. However, the more accomplished and experienced the wrestlers are, the more difficult it becomes to secure a fall. Perfecting takedown skills in wrestling is the first step toward becoming a champion wrestler.

No student of the sport would disagree with the premise that takedowns are the name of the game in wrestling. In fact, it has been statistically shown that the wrestler who scores the first takedown usually wins the match (about 85 percent of the time).

Thus, the beginning of your season (after a proper conditioning period) should be devoted primarily to takedown instruction. It has always been my contention that 70 percent of drill work before the competitive phase of the program should concentrate on takedowns. By midseason, wrestlers should spend about 50 percent of their practice time on their feet.

The components of takedown wrestling often take more time to cultivate than mat wrestling. To have success in this area, a basic philosophy of attacking and counterattacking must be developed and followed. A good takedown wrestler must be able to move his feet gracefully, constantly maintaining a good base (or center of gravity), as well as step in and penetrate his opponent's defenses.

At the same time, the wrestler must know instinctively how to finish the attack and be prepared to defend against all types of attacks executed by his opponent. The drills in this chapter focus on controlling and clearing the tie-up position for offensive takedown attacks and basic defensive counterattacks and strategies.

TAKEDOWN DRILLS

These drills are for close-contact wrestling and teach reaction maneuvers when the opponent puts "hands on" or moves out of position. The wrestler performing the drill should always start with his head up, hips (center of gravity) down, elbows in, and knees bent. In every drill, each wrestler takes turns being the drill partner.

LIFTING

Setup

W1 positions his right ear on the back of W2's spine. His left arm goes deep through the back of W2's crotch while his right hand grips under the left arm toward the back (*a*).

Action

W1 then squats in good position and explodes up to lift W2 off the mat (*b*). W1 repeats the drill several times on both sides of the partner's body.

Coaching Point

This drill teaches the proper technique for lifting an opponent off the mat. You must always stress this point.

Common Error

Never stay down on the mat after a double- or single-leg attack.

SINGLE-LEG TO DOUBLE-LEG ATTACK

Setup

W1 shoots a single-leg when W2 reaches for W1 (*a* and *b*).

Action

W2's responsibility is to sprawl back so that W1 must switch from a single-leg to a double before driving W2 to the mat (*c*). W1 must change to a double as quickly as possible.

Coaching Points

The emphasis of these drills is to promote the importance of lowering the hips and penetrating the opponent's defense. The wrestlers must learn to react to the opponent's change of stance by changing attack from single-leg to double-leg immediately.

Common Error

Don't let wrestlers stay on the knee too long without quickly driving into the double-leg.

DOUBLE-LEG ATTACK

Setup

W1 starts with a double-leg position on W2 as W2 reaches for W1 (*a*).

Action

As W2 sprawls back, W1 lifts W2's right leg up, driving his head into W2's side (*b*). As W1 continues driving his head into W2's side, W1 also blocks W2's left leg with his right arm. W1 finishes the double takedown by lifting W2's leg higher, forcing W2's body to the side with his head and driving W2 to the mat (*c*).

Coaching Points

Emphasize the importance of the offensive wrestler lifting the defensive wrestler's leg as high as possible while using his head to assist in driving the defensive wrestler to the side before taking him to the mat. The offensive wrestler cannot hesitate when executing this highly effective takedown.

Common Error

Don't let wrestlers stay on the knee while attempting the double.

DOUBLE-LEG TO SINGLE-LEG

Setup

W1 starts with a double-leg on W2 (*a*).

Action

W1 loses control of W2's right leg as W2 sprawls his leg away. W1 then attacks W2's left leg with his right arm while grasping his right wrist with his left hand (*b*). In this position, either W1 can turn the corner and drive through W2, capturing his far knee, or W1 can quickly stand up, controlling W2's leg, before performing the single-leg takedown.

Coaching Point

This situation drill teaches adjusting the wrestler's position from the double-leg attack, changing to a single-leg attack. Keep the wrestlers aware of this point so they learn to change tactics when appropriate.

Common Error

As mentioned previously with double- or single-leg takedowns, the attacking wrestler should not stay on his knees, but come up as quickly as possible.

47

DOUBLE-LEG TRIP

Setup

W2 reaches for W1 in the neutral position (*a*).

Action

W1 deeply penetrates W2's defenses, hooking W2's right leg with his left leg while shooting the double-leg takedown (*b*). As they drop to the mat, W1 quickly releases his arms around W2's legs as he prepares to adjust to a ride or pinning combination (*c*).

Coaching Points

The wrestlers must be taught not to allow their upper body to trail their trip leg, or they will be placed in an off-balance position. Emphasis should also be on whipping the trip leg back as they shoulder drive through their opponents for the double-leg takedown.

Common Error

A very common mistake is that the attacking wrestler does not drive his shoulder into his opponent's mid-section while driving him to his back.

DOUBLE-LEG DRIVE-THROUGH WHEN OPPONENT REACHES

Setup

W1 is in proper attack position when W2 reaches or rises up out of the proper neutral position for defending a takedown (*a*).

Action

W1 quickly lowers his center of gravity and penetrates into W2's hips, grasping behind his knees (*b*). W1 finishes the drill by driving through W2, bringing him to the mat (*c*).

Coaching Point

The wrestlers must learn to react quickly for the takedown when an opponent places himself out of proper position and reaches in the neutral position.

Common Error

Wrestlers can have a tendency to not lower the hips before penetrating the opponent for the takedown.

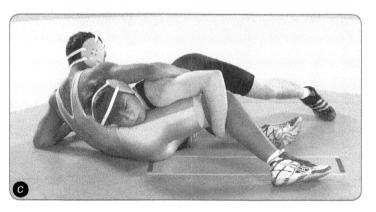

INSIDE ARM-DRAG
TO DOUBLE-LEG DRIVE-THROUGH

Setup

W2 grabs W1's wrist on the trail-leg side (*a*).

Action

W1 rotates his wrist inward and downward across his body. He also grabs above W2's elbow, completing the arm-drag and stepping into the double-leg drive-through position (*b* and *c*).

Coaching Points

The wrestlers must understand the need to tightly control the opponent's arm above the elbow when committing to the inside arm-drag while shooting the double-leg. Also, stress the point of penetrating deeply on the double-leg.

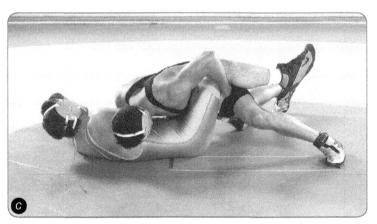

OUTSIDE ARM-DRAG
TO DOUBLE-LEG DRIVE-THROUGH

Setup

W2 makes contact by using a collar tie-up on W1's trail-leg side.

Action

W1 then controls the collar tie-up elbow, and his other hand grasps W2's far wrist (*a*). W1 then steps back, rolling W2's elbow and wrist off his head. At the same time, W1 drags W2's arm across and between both of their bodies toward W2's far knee (*b*). W1 shoots through W2 for the double-leg takedown (*c* and *d*).

Coaching Points

Always emphasize the importance of tight arm control for scoring an arm-drag to double-leg takedown. Also, stress the point of penetrating deeply on the double-leg.

ELBOW PULL AND INSIDE SINGLE-LEG TO DOUBLE-LEG DRIVE-THROUGH

Setup

W2 controls the collar and attempts to snap down W1 (*a*).

Action

W1 then lifts W2's elbow over his shoulder, shooting an inside single-leg (*b*). As W2 sprawls, W1 switches off to a double-leg drive-through takedown (*c* and *d*).

Coaching Points

As always, emphasize the importance of penetrating or driving through an opponent to score the double-leg takedown. Furthermore, stress using the head to help in driving the opponent to the mat.

ELBOW BLOCK
TO DOUBLE-LEG DRIVE-THROUGH

Setup

W2 places his hand on W1's shoulder (*a*).

Action

W1 goes into motion, driving off his trail leg. W1 uses the elbow-block technique with his thumb inside of W2's elbow when he pops W2's elbow up (*b*). At the same time, W1 lowers his level (center of gravity), makes the step between W2's feet, and executes the double-leg (*c*).

Coaching Points

This drill continues to promote the importance of changing hip position (lowering the center of gravity) in order to penetrate through an opponent for the double-leg takedown. It also stresses the point of taking advantage of an opponent's mistake with quick reaction skills.

Common Error

As mentioned previously, a common mistake by the attacking wrestler is not lowering his hips as he pops his opponent's elbow.

ELBOW HEAD PULL TO SINGLE-LEG

Setup

W2 is in the collar-tie position.

Action

W1 controls the elbow of W2's collar-tie arm and pulls the elbow from his shoulder while grabbing his opposite wrist (*a*). W1 then lowers his center of gravity, wrapping his arms around W2's leg on the side of the collar tie (*b*). He then controls the leg by lifting it high and driving W2 backward to the mat (*c* and *d*).

Coaching Points

Wrist control and lowering the center of gravity (hips) are essential factors in executing this drill. Also, make sure the wrestler has tight ankle control of his opponent's leg.

SHRUG

Setup

W2 uses a collar tie on W1's lead-leg side, while W1 controls W2's opposite wrist (*a*).

Action

W1 shrugs his shoulder and drives W2's head down while grabbing his collar-tie wrist to force it off his neck (*b*). At the same time, W1 drives W2's head down to the mat for the takedown (*c* and *d*).

Coaching Points

Wrist control and shoulder shrug quickness must be stressed during this drill. Finish the move by forcing the opponent's head down toward the mat.

FIREMAN'S CARRY

Setup

W2 underhooks W1 on his lead-leg side (*a*).

Action

W1 immediately forces the underhook elbow inward. As W2 pushes his elbow out, W1 lowers his center of gravity and shoots between the legs on his knees, wrapping his free arm around W2's leg on the side where W2 had the underhook (*b*). Tilting his shoulders away from W2's leg, W1 then whips W2 to the mat, driving his free arm through the air in the same direction for the takedown (*c* and *d*).

Coaching Point

It is very important that wrestlers control the opponent's underhook arm, tightly grabbing it above the elbow, when performing the fireman's carry and bringing the opponent to the mat.

Common Error

A common mistake is not whipping the leg-hold arm across the opponent's lower back to assist in completing the fireman's carry.

OPPOSITE-LEG FIREMAN'S CARRY

Setup

This takedown drill is a combination of the fireman's carry and elbow head pull to single-leg drills previously discussed in the chapter.

Action

W1 controls W2's underhook in the same manner as in the fireman's carry drill while grabbing the far wrist (*a*). Stepping to the outside of the opposite leg as in a single-leg attack, W1 pulls W2's arm across his body and sweeps in for a single-leg on the opposite side around the knee (*b*). Controlling the underhook arm and driving it down, W1 sits through with the leg that is on W2's underhook side to finish the takedown (*c*).

Coaching Points

As with the fireman's carry drill, emphasize a tight grip above the opponent's underhook elbow. Also, stress the importance to W1 of lowering his center of gravity (hips) when ducking his head under the opponent's arm.

SINGLE-LEG ATTACK FROM OPPONENT'S UNDERHOOK

Setup

W2 secures an underhook tie-up on the side of W1's lead leg (*a*).

Action

Pummeling the underhook arm and popping it up, W1 lowers his center of gravity while sweeping his arm around W2's lead leg, picking it up and bringing W2 to the mat (*b* and *c*).

Coaching Points

Highlight the significance of quickly lowering the center of gravity (hips) as the wrestler single-leg sweeps his opponent during the drill. Also, make sure the wrestler has tight ankle control of his opponent's leg.

SIDE HEADLOCK

Setup

This drill starts in a situation where W2 is able to elevate W1's elbow with his underhook (*a*).

Action

As W2 elevates W1's elbow, W1 steps between W2's legs and then headlocks and hips his partner to the mat, controlling W2's far arm above the elbow (*b* and *c*).

Coaching Points

This drill should be taught as a desperation move for a situation in which a match is nearing the end, and the wrestler is behind by three or more points. Wrestlers must have a few strategies for this type of situation. It is important that the attacker keep his hips (or center of gravity) low when performing this takedown.

SINGLE-LEG SWEEP

Setup

W1 is in the traditional breakdown position facing W2 but not tying up with him.

Action

W1 quickly fakes a single-leg attack to W2's left angle, slapping his right hand on the mat (*a*). This maneuver causes W2 to step his left leg back. Next, W1 sweeps to W2's right ankle and picks it up (*b* and *c*). Finally, W1 forward trips W2's left leg above the knee, forcing W2 to the mat (*d*).

Coaching Points

It is imperative to stress that your wrestlers quickly change direction and sweep low on their opponents' ankles. Furthermore, they must also be instructed to stand up with the leg (ankle trapped with the left hand) as quickly as possible so they don't get stuck down on the mat. Of course, the single-leg sweep can also be performed on the opposite leg as well. This is a drill that can generally be taught to a youth wrestler who has been involved with wrestling for two years or more.

Common Error

Wrestlers will grasp the leg above the ankle and maneuver too slowly to the feet after sweeping the single leg.

60 DRILL

CROSS-ANKLE PICK

Setup

W1 applies the collar-biceps tie-up without his head against W2's head.

Action

W1 quickly steps to the side and then drops to the mat. This maneuver forces W2's head down and left foot to step forward. W1 then grasps W2's left ankle with his left hand while forcing W2's head down toward W2's left knee (*a* and *b*). Finally, W1 pulls W2's left ankle out and up (high) while pushing W2's head down and back, forcing him off balance and to the mat (*c*). Note: Upon scoring the takedown, W2 is vulnerable to W1 applying the cradle pinning combination.

Coaching Points

When demonstrating the cross-ankle pick, be sure to stress the following points. First, your wrestlers must swiftly step to the side and drop to the mat. Second, they should be aware of the importance of pulling their opponent's head to his knee. Finally, you need to emphasize to your wrestlers that they pick the ankle up as high off the mat as possible, driving backward and forcing opponents to the mat.

BARREL ROLL (OR DUMP)

Setup

W1 executes a double-leg takedown, and W2 counters by sprawling but misses the cross-face and underhooks W1's left shoulder.

Action

W1 tightly grabs W2's underhook above the elbow with his left hand while blocking the outside of W2's right leg with his right hand (*a*). Next, W1 pulls W2's underhook down while sitting through with his left leg (*b*). Then W1 finishes the barrel roll by sliding his head across W2's chest and ending in the pancake position (*c*), as detailed in chapter 4.

Coaching Points

When you teach the barrel roll, you must stress three important points. First, the wrestler must have a very tight grip on his opponent's underhook arm. Second, he has to block his opponent's right leg with his own right arm. This action will help to put his opponent off balance. Finally, you must instruct the wrestler to tuck the underhook arm against his chest while hitting a quick sit-through to secure the takedown.

Common Error

The attacker doesn't keep a tight hold on the opponent's elbow while initiating the move.

DUCK-UNDER

Setup

W1 waits for W2 to reach for his collar.

Action

As W2 reaches for W1's collar, W1 pops the arm up and lowers his center of gravity (*a*). W1 then pressures the back of W2's arm with his head and spins behind (*b*). W1 finishes the maneuver by forward tripping W2 to the mat (*c*).

Coaching Point

Although the forward trip was used to finish the move, your wrestlers may have another wrestling variation to finish the takedown, such as the backward trip.

Common Errors

Mistakes include not lowering the hips or bending the head down.

UNDERHOOK TO CROSS-ANKLE PICK

Setup

W1 underhooks W2's near arm with his head blocking W2's head to gain inside control.

Action

W1 trips W2's near leg, lifting it off the mat and backward (*a*). W1 then drops to the mat, pulling W2's underhooked shoulder toward the mat. At the same time, W1 grasps W2's far ankle (*b*). W1 finishes the maneuver by pulling up W2's far ankle and driving into W2 (who is off balance), forcing W2 to the mat (*c*).

Coaching Points

Your wrestlers must be taught the importance of tripping their opponent's near leg as high as possible to the rear. Likewise, they need to force the opponent's underhooked shoulder down as they drop to the mat. Finally, they should grab the far ankle as low as they can while driving into their opponent, finishing the maneuver.

Common Errors

Mistakes include not tripping the opponent's leg high and not forcing the underhook shoulder to the mat.

TAKEDOWN COUNTER DRILLS

The premise for takedown counter drills is to stop your opponent's initial attack and then create a counterattack in which you score. This is best accomplished by keeping in good position with a proper center-of-gravity (hip) location. In other words, do not allow your opponent to feel comfortable in the neutral position when he attempts takedown maneuvers.

Keep in mind that the fundamentals must be taught first, including conventional sprawling drills, proper crossface techniques and hip-positioning drills, and whizzer-hip counter drills to double-leg attacks. Also, review all single-leg counter maneuvers when the attack wrestler has control of the leg on or off the mat. Wrestlers must master these basic drills before they learn the more advanced takedown counter drills.

The following drill sequence is set up to demonstrate the first line of defense drills, using the hands to prevent your opponent from penetrating to the legs. The second line of defense drills will illustrate techniques used when the opponent is able to penetrate to the legs or body by maneuvering through the first line of defense.

SNAP-DOWN REDIRECT

Setup

W1 controls W2's head with a collar tie with his right arm. W1 also establishes wrist control with his left hand and arm (*a*).

Action

As W2 begins his attempt to penetrate W1, W1 snaps his head and elbows to the mat while sprawling back. Pressing his chest on W2's back, W1 drives W2's head to the mat, blocking W2's right arm (*b*). Finally, W1 spins around W2 for the takedown (*c*).

Coaching Point

When the wrestlers sprawl, stress the importance of sprawling on the toes and placing pressure on the opponent's back before spinning around.

Common Error

A common mistake is the attacker dropping to his knees rather than staying on his toes when snapping the opponent down.

SNAP-DOWN TO SHUCK

Setup

This drill is a variation of the snap-down redirect drill, except for the reaction by W1. From the collar tie, as W2 attempts to shoot a double-leg, W1 snaps his partner's head down (*a*).

Action

W1 shucks W2's head to the side, driving his collar-tie elbow across the chin, creating an angle to spin behind W2 and score the defensive takedown (*b-d*).

Coaching Point

Emphasize that the wrestlers must use a quick whipping motion during the shuck before spinning behind.

Common Error

A common mistake would be W1 dropping to his knees while attempting to go behind his opponent.

Variation

Other variations would include snapping the attacking (double-leg) wrestler's head down with either elbow and spinning behind in either the left or right direction.

FRONT HEADLOCK TO BUTT-DRAG

Setup

This counter drill is used when W2 attempts a double-leg from the open position stance (*a*).

Action

W1 reacts by sprawling back, locking his arms around W2's head and shoulder, and lowering his hips (*b*). As W2 is forced to the mat, W1 (with his head under W2's chest) wraps his arm around W2's leg while circling to his left and forcing W2's head in the same direction (*c*). At the same time, W1 drives into W2 with his head, forcing W2 off his base and scoring the countertakedown (*d*).

Coaching Point

This drill must be performed with proper and assertive circular motion, forcing the opponent's head in the same direction.

Variation

When possible, wrestlers can execute a near-side cradle.

FRONT HEADLOCK TO SHUCK

Setup

The wrestlers are in the same headlock position as the previous drill.

Action

W1 forces W2's head toward the mat (*a*). As W2 begins to push his head up, W1 shucks, whipping W2's head away from him (*b*). This allows W1 to attack W2's side for the countertakedown (*c*).

Coaching Point

The emphasis in this drill is the importance of proper head pressure before shucking the opponent's head away and attacking the side for the takedown.

Common Error

The attacker does not whip his opponent's head hard enough when performing the shuck.

FRONT HEADLOCK
TO CROSS-ANKLE CRADLE

Setup

W1 starts from the front headlock counter position.

Action

W1 stays on his toes and forces W2's head to the mat (*a*). After driving W2's head to the mat, W1 reaches for the cross ankle with his left hand, pulling it toward W2's head (*b*). W1 finishes the move by thrusting into W2 and quickly executing an inside-leg cradle (*c*).

Coaching Point

Emphasize the importance of placing pressure on the opponent's ankle when grabbing the cross ankle so he cannot move it when initiating the drill.

DOUBLE-LEG REACTION COUNTER

Setup

The wrestlers are in the open stance position.

Action

W2 attempts a double-leg and is blocked by W1 (*a*). As W2 adjusts by attempting to regain his original takedown position, W1 immediately reacts with a counterattack double-leg takedown (*b* and *c*).

Coaching Points

Stress the significance of not only countering but quickly attacking offensively, not being satisfied with just blocking an attack. This is also an opportune time to finish by driving an opponent to his back with a half nelson.

Variation

Should the opponent shoot the double-leg with his head down, a variation would be to snap his head down with either elbow and spin behind.

DOUBLE-LEG WHIZZER COUNTER

Setup

W2 shoots a double-leg takedown with W1 sprawling and overhooking the near arm to initiate the whizzer (*a*).

Action

W1 initiates the whizzer and pops his hip into W2, driving W2's head toward the mat (*b*). W1 finishes the counter by forcing W2's head to the mat with his free hand while sprawling away and facing W2 (*c*).

Coaching Points

Two points must be stressed when applying the whizzer. First, the whizzer must be driven with force so that the drill wrestler's shoulder is above his opponent's shoulder. Second, when popping the near hip into the drill partner to break the double-leg grip, the drill wrestler should not prolong the pressure on his opponent's body because the drill partner could roll through and score the takedown. In other words, pop the hip and quickly release to break the double-leg grip.

Common Error

A common mistake is not popping the hip with extreme force and driving the whizzer with as much power as possible.

HIP-HEIST SINGLE-LEG COUNTER

Setup

The purpose of this drill is to teach the wrestlers how to get off their hips when an opponent is close to securing a single takedown. Start the drill with W2 controlling one leg with his head to the outside of W1.

Action

In this position, W1 lifts his outside hip and grabs W2's near-side buttock (a). Next, W1 hip-heists his inside leg through while pulling W2's body forward with the buttock hand and posting his free arm on the mat for the counterscore (b and c).

Coaching Point

A great prerequisite activity for this counter drill is the hip-heist drill, explained in more detail as a solitary drill in chapter 8. It promotes proper technique in executing the hip heist.

SINGLE-LEG COUNTER

Setup

This drill starts with W2 executing a single-leg, lifting it off the mat (*a*).

Action

From this position, W1 must force his head inside, grab W2's outside wrist, and secure a whizzer with his inside arm (*b*). W1 must then work his captured leg to the outside and sprawl it back while driving the whizzer forward and popping his hips into W2 (*c*). W1 can finish the maneuver by forcing W2 to the mat and spinning behind him for the countertakedown.

Coaching Point

The wrestlers must learn to whizzer with pressure while sprawling and forcing the hips into the opponent to succeed in the countertakedown.

Common Error

Not driving the whizzer forward in a forceful manner is a common problem.

SINGLE-LEG SPLADDLE COUNTER

Setup

W2 shoots a single-leg takedown with his head inside and on both his knees (*a*).

Action

W1 reacts by pressuring W2's head and back to the mat, stepping his lead foot inside W2's calf, and locking his hands around W2's outside leg (*b*). W1 finishes the counter by dropping to his inside hip and forcing W2's back to the mat for the takedown, near-fall points, and possibly a fall (*c*).

Coaching Points

It is very important that the drill wrestler keep his weight on his lead leg. The drill wrestler must also keep his body pressure on the drill partner so he cannot come to his feet. This weight pressure will also force the drill partner into a ball position, with his head in front of his legs in preparation for the spladdle. After mastering the spladdle, the wrestlers realize the importance of immediately standing up when executing a single-leg to avoid being spladdled.

CONCLUSION

Developing and using a proper system of takedown drills is the most essential element in becoming a successful takedown artist. The more a skill is repeated correctly, the more firmly it becomes established as an automatic move that is very effective against an opponent.

During competition, action occurs too quickly for the wrestler to stop and think about what to do or how to do it. In wrestling, he who hesitates loses. For this very reason, the wrestler must be willing to invest hours upon hours performing takedown and takedown counter drills.

Once your wrestlers progress in their takedown skills, they are ready to be introduced to more complex takedown maneuvers. In chapter 4, they will be exposed to advanced throws and takedowns that will add to their takedown arsenal.

Advanced Throws and Takedowns

Larry Shaw and Bill Welker

" *The world is moving so fast these days that the man who says it can't be done is generally interrupted by someone doing it.* "

Elbert Hubbard

ADVANCED THROWS

The throw is one of the most explosive and exciting techniques that a wrestler can execute against his opponent. A well-timed throw can change the course of a wrestling match in the blink of an eye. Not only can a wrestler earn a quick five points (takedown and near fall), he can end the match in dramatic fashion by securing a fall with a successful throw.

While most wrestlers spend a large portion of their time drilling double- and single-leg takedowns, they should also spend time developing the skills for throwing an opponent. By rehearsing the various controls, angles, pressure, lifting, and arching positions, a wrestler can have the confidence to throw from a variety of positions when the moment presents itself. *Advanced throws are very effective maneuvers for the higher weight classes as well.*

The opportunity to hit a throw may only occur a few times during a season, but that opportunity might occur at a match-changing moment. Even if your wrestlers have no intention of ever using a throw in a match, it is critical that they practice these positions so that they can instantly recognize them and be able to prevent becoming a victim of this devastatingly effective technique.

Prior to teaching advanced throws, you must teach your wrestlers the skills that will prepare them for performing advanced throw techniques. Coach Larry Shaw takes you step-by-step through those drills.

Prethrow Takedown Skills

1. Pummeling

Wrestlers must master this skill and its options before they can become competent in upper-body wrestling. Begin with each wrestler in a face-to-face

position with each wrestler having an overhook and an underhook. Each wrestler will attempt to force his overhook arm into an underhook while keeping his elbows in contact with his body.

They should be placed in a standing position with their hips back. Finally, the drill should be executed with the wrestlers moving their feet. It's important that, as the wrestler moves his overhook to an underhook, he also force his shoulder into his opponent's chest, thereby maintaining an angle in relation to his opponent's body. A variation would be pummeling on their knees, especially with youth wrestlers.

2. Wall Walk

The wrestler stands with his back approximately 2 feet (60 cm) away from a padded wall. The wrestler arches back into the wall, placing his palms against the wall with fingers facing downward (*a*). He then walks his hands down the wall until his head touches, or nearly touches, the wrestling mat (*b* and *c*). Finally, he walks his hands back up the wall until he is in an upright position.

Make sure that the wrestler maintains an arched position throughout. This activity can be done a specific number of repetitions or as a timed activity.

3. Hand-Held Arch

The wrestlers face each other; W2 supports W1 with an interlocking grip (*a*). W1 steps with his inside foot to the outside of W2's foot (*b*). He then steps with his outside foot so that his feet are parallel. Once in that position W1 squats down, lowering his center of gravity (*c*). He arches back and forces his hips up (*d*), turning to his outside shoulder as he contacts the wrestling mat. He then turns out to a base position.

W1 should be instructed to use a step—step—squat—arch—turn sequence. As he is executing the drill, W1 focuses first on a wall, then the ceiling, and finally the wall behind him before turning as he contacts the wrestling mat.

Wrestlers need to be reminded not to turn too quickly. After a wrestler has mastered this with a partner, he can then do it without a partner by following each step in the sequence.

4. Body Lock Stepping the Corner

The wrestlers face one another in the pummeling position as W1 creates an angle to W2 by stepping to his underhook side and pulling W2's triceps (*a*). He then steps the corner, attacking W2's underhook side. He places his foot behind W2's heel and locks his hand on W2's far hip (*b*). Dropping his center of gravity, W1 drives his hips into W2's hip. W1 lifts W2 and carries him two or three steps (*c*), and then setting him back on his feet.

W1 needs to be perpendicular to W2. He must maintain a good wrestler's stance to be able to generate the lifting power to throw W2.

5. Back Step

The wrestler faces the wall in a square stance with his palms on the wall. The wrestler does a cross step, placing his heel about a foot in front of his toe (*a*). He does a back step with his other foot, placing his toe behind his heel (*b*). This action creates a pivot point. He drops his center of gravity and rotates his back to the wall, driving his hips to a higher level (*c*).

This activity teaches the wrestler the importance of getting his feet and hips in the proper position to have the most lift and power to execute many throws. It's important to emphasize the cross-step and back-step action, along with the concept of changing levels (going under the table) when pivoting his back to the wall.

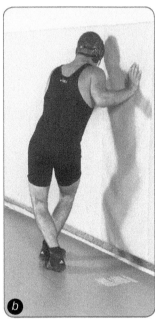

ADVANCED THROW
TAKEDOWN DRILLS

Having perfected the preceding skills, your wrestlers are ready to learn advanced throw techniques. As my coauthor, Bill Welker, emphasizes later in the chapter, all wrestlers must first have a firm background regarding single- and double-leg takedown attacks before attempting his pancake takedown series.

The following advanced throws offer wrestlers another avenue to taking their opponents to the mat, with the strong possibility of scoring points for a near fall or a fall. Study the mechanics and the significance of teaching advanced throws to your more experienced wrestlers very carefully. They will benefit from such instruction.

UNDERARM SPIN

Setup

The wrestlers face each other in the pummeling position.

Action

W1 pinches W2's underhook as he does a side step to create an angle. He then taps W2's leg with his overhook hand (*a*). W2 steps the tapped leg back, opening up his underhook side. W1 then steps through (using the step–step technique from the hand-held arch drill) bringing his underhook arm across and up into W2's armpit (*b*). W1 then arches back and finishes the throw by sweeping his arm across W2's body to prevent him from scooting off his back (*c* and *d*).

Coaching Points

The side step is very important; it allows W1 to create the proper attack angle. Make sure that W1 completes the arch before turning out to complete the throw properly.

DOUBLE OVERHOOK

Setup

W1 has double overhooks, and W2 has double underhooks with his hands locked.

Action

W1 lets W2 pull his body into W2's chest after briefly resisting by keeping his hips back (*a*). W1 uses the step, step, squat, arch, turn technique from the hand-held arch drill to execute this throw (*b* and *c*).

Coaching Points

W1 needs to step between W2's feet to be in the proper position to be able to generate the explosive power to execute this throw. This throw can be used as an arching drill by having W2 place his palms against W1's back and doing a forward roll (W2 needs to keep his head tucked) as W1 arches and finishes the throw.

BODY LOCK THROW

Setup

The wrestlers face one another in the pummeling position.

Action

W1 steps to his underhook side while pulling W2's arm with his overhook hand (*a*). This creates an angle that allows W1 to step the corner and pinch W2's underhook by locking his hands on W2's far hip or lower back (*b*). W1 then drops his center of gravity , drives his hips through W2's, arches, and turns to his near shoulder, taking W2 to his back (*c*). W1 needs to quickly scissor his legs to finish in a chest-to-chest position (*d*).

Coaching Points

W1 needs to control W2 throughout the lift and arch positions to avoid being called for an illegal slam. For this throw to be successful, W2 must be pressuring into W1. If W1 doesn't feel any pressure, he should change direction, pinch W2's near leg, sag him to the mat, and finish as if he had thrown W2.

BODY LOCK STEER THROW

Setup

The wrestlers are in the body-lock throw position (*a*).

Action

W2 keeps his hips back to prevent W1 from stepping behind his near leg to gain the throwing position. W1 reacts by stepping across W2's body (*b*) and then throws W2 to the front (*c* and *d*).

Coaching Points

W1 needs to make sure that W2's upper body is in a forward-leaning position. As he steps across W2's body, W1 must keep his feet close together to generate the power through his hips to take W2 across his body to his back.

HIP TOSS

Setup

The wrestlers face each other in the pummeling position.

Action

W1 moves to his overhook side while using his underhook to pull W2 and create an angle on that side (*a*). He then bumps his underhook up, drops his hand, and catches W2's far hip (*b*). He steps through in front of W2's lap and loads W2 across his hip while pulling W2's arm (controlling the triceps) across, creating a rotating action of W2's upper body (*c*), and throwing him to his back (*d*).

Coaching Points

To execute this throw properly, W1 must create an angle so that he can step through and load W2 on his hip. W1 must also keep his feet under his hips so that he can generate the power to throw W2.

OPEN HEADLOCK

Setup

The wrestlers face one another in the pummeling position.

Action

W1 allows W2 to pummel his overhook into an underhook. Instead of pummeling back to an underhook, W1 drives his shoulder into W2's sternum while circling his head with the overhook arm on that side (*a*). W1 pulls W2's near-side underhook arm tight (*b*), using a back-step technique to rotate his body away from W2 (*c*). He then drives his hips into W2 and finishes the throw, taking W2 to his back (*d*).

Coaching Point

W1 needs to feel pressure from W2, making sure that he can quickly step back and rotate his hips underneath W2's lap.

CLOSED HEADLOCK

Setup

The wrestlers face one another in the pummeling position.

Action

As he does in the open headlock position, W1 allows W2 to pummel into an underhook so that W1 can use his overhook to attack W2's head. However, to get into the closed headlock position, W1 must pummel into an underhook on the other side (*a*). W1 then forces his underhook up so that he can lock his hands behind W2's neck (*b*). To finish, W1 throws W2 to his underhook side by rotating his upper body to that side as he steps across W2's body (*c* and *d*).

Coaching Point

It's important that W1 quickly change direction to force W2's weight on to his outside foot.

REVERSE HEADLOCK

Setup

The wrestlers face one another in the pummeling position.

Action

W1 secures a closed headlock. In this situation, W2 has eliminated W1's throwing angle and has blocked W1 from stepping in by posting his hip (a). W1 reacts by driving his lock behind W2's neck and shifting his chest into W2 (b). W1 then rotates his lock and forces W2 to the mat on his opposite side (c and d).

Coaching Points

As W1 is taking W2 to the mat, he needs to step out to the throw side to ensure that he lands in a perpendicular position to W2. W1 needs to make sure that, as he rotates his upper body, he is forcing W2's weight onto his outside foot. This is a great position from which W1 can incorporate a foot block with his outside foot, preventing W2 from stepping to that side to prevent the throw from being executed.

METZGER

Setup

The wrestlers face one another in the pummeling position.

Action

W1 drives his underhook arm up to raise W2's overhook side. He then does a side step to get W2 to step forward while creating an attack angle. Finally, W1 forces his overhook down and takes his hand through W2's crotch (*a*) while stepping behind W2's outside heel (*b*). To finish W1 uses his chest to drive W2 to the mat (*c*).

Coaching Points

This drill is a must for every wrestler who finds himself in an upper-body tie-up. This technique can be used to defend a lateral drop attempt by controlling the throwing wrestler's hips.

a

b

c

THE PANCAKE TAKEDOWN SERIES

Bill Welker's pancake takedown series is a neutral position maneuver that very few wrestling authors have given attention to over the years. However, many wrestlers have found it to be a very effective maneuver at the scholastic, collegiate, and international levels. Ironically, this series has been a part of wrestling for centuries. Why there has never been any detailed description of the various pancake takedowns is a puzzle. Even one of the best-selling contemporary wrestling books, *Winning Wrestling Moves* by Mark Mysnyk et al. (1994), barely broaches the topic of the pancake takedown series. The remainder of this chapter describes in detail the pancake takedown series and its significance in the sport of wrestling.

To begin with, you must fully understand that the pancake takedown is a technical maneuver, not a muscle move. In fact, you are often using your opponent's momentum to catch him off balance and take him to the mat. Furthermore, it's a takedown tactic that can score multiple points for your wrestler. Finally, the pancake takedown is a dynamic move for wrestlers of all shapes and sizes—lightweights, middleweights, and heavyweights.

During my competitive days, I successfully executed the pancake takedown in numerous matches. To be honest, I referred to it as my "element of surprise" takedown. Every great wrestler knows, first and foremost, he must perfect his single- and double-leg takedowns. They are the "bread and butter" takedowns in wrestling. But these same championship wrestlers also perfect a third takedown maneuver such as a duck-under, arm drag, fireman's carry, or shrug. The pancake takedown was my very effective surprise trick move in competition. With practice, it can be your wrestlers' third takedown as well.

Pre-Pancake Takedown Series Skills

Before teaching your wrestlers the various pancake takedowns, you must expose them to the skills necessary for properly executing this unique takedown.

1. Pancake-On-Knees Balance

This drill is introduced to the wrestlers to put them into the correct down-on-their-knees pancake position. The wrestlers are placed in the overhook and underhook situation with their heads on the overhook side. On the whistle, the wrestlers attempt to force their partner off balance and take him to the mat on his back. Important note: After hitting the pancake, the top wrestler should always be perpendicular to the bottom wrestler. The wrestlers have 15 seconds from the whistle to perform the maneuver.

2. Standing Pancake Balance

This drill is introduced to the wrestlers to put them into the correct standing pancake position. The wrestlers are placed in the overhook and underhook situation with their heads on the overhook side. On the whistle, the wrestlers attempt to force their partner off balance and take him to the mat on his back. The drill should be performed in groups so there is enough room, and the wrestlers aren't bumping into each other. The wrestlers have 15 seconds from the whistle to perform the maneuver.

3. Post-Pancake Pinning

After executing the pancake takedown, the wrestlers must correctly position themselves. When the bottom wrestler turns into them, the top wrestler should scissor his legs to the belly-down position on their toes, driving into his opponent (*a*). Should the bottom wrestler turn away from them, the top wrestler must scissor his legs to the belly-up position, sagging back on his hips (*b*). On the whistle, the bottom wrestler turns in, and the top wrestler scissors to the proper position. When the whistle is blown again, the bottom wrestler turns out, while the top wrestler readjusts to the correct position. This would be a 15- to 30-second whistle drill for each wrestler.

4. Balance Check

This drill is an offshoot of the pancake takedown. It's performed with the wrestlers on their knees, the offensive wrestler in the collar and biceps tie-up, with defensive wrestler mistakenly sitting on his feet and shins (*a*). At this point, the offensive wrestler drives his collar arm into the defensive wrestler's chest, forcing his back and shoulders to the mat (*b*). Note: When the defensive wrestler is on his back, the offensive wrestler readjusts to the overhook and underhook pancake position.

Pancake Takedown Series Drills

Once you have taught your wrestlers the various prepancake drills, they are equipped to learn the pancake takedown series. Keep in mind, as with all takedown strategies, the pancake takedown series may not suit the individual style of every team member. Still, once wrestlers are made aware of its effectiveness, they may use it by instinct during competition because of practice drill work.

In fact, although my brother, Floyd Welker, was a double leg and fireman's carry artist, it was his introduction to the pancake takedown series that taught him to hit a lateral drop (standing pancake), winning his state championship match. With that said, carefully study the following pancake takedown series drills.

PANCAKE OFF THE DOUBLE-LEG (WIDE ELBOWS) ATTACK

Setup

W1 is in the breakdown position while W2 attempts a double-leg takedown with elbows open wide.

Action

W1 lowers his hips and applies the overhook and underhook with his head on the overhook side (*a*). Next, using W2's momentum, W1 pancakes W2 by driving his underhook arm across W2's chest to the side and taking W2 to the mat on his back (*b*).

Coaching Points

It is important that you make sure the wrestlers finish the pancake perpendicular to the bottom. Also, see to it that the wrestlers tighten their overhook and underhook arms. After the pancake, the wrestlers could also readjust by switching to a half nelson and crotch or a cradle.

PANCAKE FROM THE WHIZZER TO QUARTER NELSON

Setup

W2 executes a double-leg takedown with elbows in the proper position. In this situation, W2 gains a tight double leg, clasping his hands behind W1's knees.

Action

As W2 has the deep double leg, W1 sprawls on his toes and applies the whizzer (*a*). W1 drives W2 down with the whizzer and then adjusts to the quarter nelson, forcing W2's head to the mat (*b*). When W2 forces his head up, W1 quickly releases the quarter nelson, lifts the whizzer arm up, steps in front of W2 and whips his free arm across W2's chest in the underhook position, pancaking W2's back to the mat (*c* and *d*).

Coaching Points

You must teach the wrestlers the proper whizzer techniques. For example, when using the whizzer, the wrestlers must learn to repeatedly pop their hips into their opponents, or they could be rolled through by their opponents. The roll through is a maneuver in which a wrestler uses his opponent's whizzer momentum to roll under him, popping the far leg and ending on top. Furthermore, your wrestlers must be made aware of the importance of having their whizzer shoulder higher than their opponents' shoulder. To give a battlefield analogy, with the whizzer, always command the high ground.

LATERAL DROP
FROM THE STAND-UP ESCAPE

Setup

W1 has just performed a stand-up escape and is facing W2. At this point, there are two possible scenarios, depending on which wrestler drives into the other immediately after the escape. Though I am going to explain what W1 should do after escaping with W2 lunging at him, the opposite could also occur if W1 drives into W2. Please keep that in mind. (Note: The lateral drop is, in reality, a standing pancake.)

Action

As W1 completes a standing escape and faces W2 (*a*), W2 charges toward him. At this point, W1 locks into an overhook and underhook lateral drop, taking W2 to his back on W2's momentum (*b*).

Coaching Points

Since this situation happens often during a match, you need to make sure that your wrestlers are exposed to such a takedown strategy. See to it your wrestlers are able to take advantage of it. The lateral drop off the stand-up is a takedown with which a wrestler can score four or five quick points, perhaps even a fall.

LATERAL DROP AS A PRIMARY TAKEDOWN

Setup
W1 quickly and forcefully works into the pancake underhook and overhook position on W2.

Action
After W1 maneuvers into the overhook and underhook on W2, W1 then shoves W2 backward. When W2 retaliates by forcing into W1 (a), W1 pancakes W2 to the mat on his back (b).

Coaching Point
First and foremost, you must fully understand that the lateral drop as a primary takedown is a *desperation* move. If W2 does not react by driving into W1, and W1 tries to force the lateral drop, W1 could easily end up on his back. It should *only* be initiated when your wrestler is losing by three or more points, and there are seconds left in the match.

Common Error
A very common mistake is to try to force the lateral drop during the match when there is no need to execute this do-or-die maneuver.

157

STANDING PANCAKE UNDERHOOK/ NEAR ANKLE TRIP

Setup

W1 underhooks W2's near arm, with W1's head blocking W2's head to gain inside control. W1 also controls W2's far wrist (or elbow) with his free hand.

Action

W1 trips W2's near ankle. At the same time, while W2 is off balance, W1 pulls W2's far arm across his chest, turning and driving W2's back toward the mat (*a* and *b*). W1 finishes the maneuver by dropping to his knees before assuming the proper pancake position (*c* and *d*).

Coaching Points

It is important to executive the takedown as forcefully as possible. However, when taking the wrestler to the mat, your wrestlers must learn to drop to their knees first, prior to readjusting into the pancake position. The reason for this is quite simple. If your wrestler hits the move and pounces on top of his opponent on the mat, the official could signal a slam.

WELKER KNEE PANCAKE

Before explaining this pancake drill, I want to share with you the origin of the maneuver. While in high school during the early 1960s, I developed and perfected (via extensive drill work) the knee pancake during practice. I was highly successful executing the knee pancake in competition. In fact, even though many of my opponents were aware of it and prepared to counter it, I still surprised them with the knee pancake during dual meet and tournament competition.

My high school wrestling coaches never taught it; I just learned to use it on my own. Since the move was fundamentally sound and not a high-risk maneuver, they had no problem accepting it as part of my takedown repertoire. In truth, the Welker knee pancake is an example of individual wrestler creativity discussed in chapter 9.

Setup

W1 underhooks W2's near arm, with W1's head blocking W2's head to gain inside control. W1 also controls W2's far wrist or above the far elbow with his free hand (*a*).

Action

In the standing underhook position controlling the far arm, W1 drops to his knees, forcing W2 down with him (*b*). W1 then pulls W2's near shoulder down with his underhook hand. W1 watches W2's near knee. When W2 lifts his knee up, even a fraction of an inch (*c*), W1 drives into W2, pulling W2's far arm across his chest and pancaking W2 to the mat (*d*).

Coaching Points

Stress the importance of keeping a firm underhook and controlling the far wrist or above the far elbow. Also, when they are down on the mat, your wrestlers should focus their attention on the opponent's near knee. The uniqueness of this maneuver is that even with the near knee just slightly off the mat, the wrestler has placed himself off-balance and is easy prey for the Welker knee pancake.

CONCLUSION

Advanced throws and takedowns add to your wrestlers' takedown arsenal. Furthermore, like the advanced pinning combination drills in chapter 7, they assist in preparing the wrestlers by introducing them to international skills in the areas of freestyle and Greco-Roman competition.

By teaching advanced throws and the pancake takedown series, you are offering your wrestlers further takedown options. Likewise, you need to demonstrate counters to such upper-body moves. If they are wrestling an opponent who is a throw or pancake performer, you must emphasize to your wrestlers that they should not tie up, or if they do, it should only be the collar and biceps tie-up to defend all throws.

Finally, if you are interested in learning more about the pancake takedown series, you can visit billwelkerwrestling.com. There you can purchase *Bill Welker's Pancake Takedown Series DVD*.

The next three chapters focus on the second phase of the sport—mat or ground wrestling. In chapter 5, you will be exposed to drill tactics in the areas of escapes and reversals, as well as their counters. This is a significant area of wrestling that in recent years has been given minor attention; don't allow your wrestlers to overlook the need for match-effective escape and reversal skills.

CHAPTER

5

Escapes
and Reversals

Pat Pecora

" *There are no shortcuts to any place worth going.* "

Beverly Sills

With so much emphasis on takedown strategies in recent decades, escape and reversal skills have been given positions of less significance during practice. This contemporary practice has had its negative effects. To the astute observer of mat wrestling, today's wrestlers do not demonstrate the flow of movement in the defensive position needed to ensure success.

Today, wrestlers attempt one or two escape or reversal moves in competition; then, if the maneuvers fail, the wrestler stops, and his opponent commences to control him. One vivid example of this problem lies in how the 30-second tiebreaker has changed over the last few years. Initially, the wrestler who chose the bottom position was very confident of escaping with a quick stand-up. That approach has been compromised.

It is time to again place more importance on the escape-and-reversal defense during the entire match. Wrestlers must be exposed to more drill instruction to improve this area of weakness, and this can be accomplished only on the practice mats.

The following drills are designed to help develop wrestlers' skills in the defensive position. Likewise, you will be exposed to escape and reversal counter drills in the offensive position.

ESCAPE AND REVERSAL DRILLS

In this section, the drills emphasize the significance of inside control as an important factor for experiencing success in the defensive position. The wrestlers are also taught that a proper base must be established to escape or reverse their opponents.

As a wrestling coach for nearly three decades, I have determined that *inside control* is the first essential principle in escapes and reversals. Inside control is often mistaken for *hand control*, which is a different tactic. Inside control involves controlling the inside of your body, not just your opponent's hands. Inside control and hand control are demonstrated repeatedly throughout the remainder of the chapter.

INSIDE CONTROL
IN THE STANDING POSITION

Setup

The drill begins in a standing position with W2 behind W1.

Action

It is important to be in good position, with W1's head up, back straight, buttocks down, elbows in, and knees bent. During inside control drills, the most important body parts for W1 range from the inside of the elbow up to the armpit. W1 gains inside control of the body by keeping the elbows firmly against his body to stop W2 from getting inside (*a*). (If W2 does get inside, W1 should use a windshield-wiper motion with the arms to regain inside control.) Having gained inside control with the arms, W1 then works on controlling W2's hand or hands (*b*). At this point, W1 cuts and escapes (*c*).

Coaching Points

The offensive wrestler's goal is to try to lock his hands around the defensive wrestler's waist or gain wrist control on the defensive wrestler. The defensive wrestler's goal is to get inside control before the offensive wrestler does. If the offensive wrestler gets inside control, start the drill over. With practice, the defensive wrestler should be able to perform this drill with his eyes closed, feeling where the offensive wrestler is at all times. The defensive wrestler must never reach with the hands to get control. This action causes the defensive wrestler's elbows to come out from his body, allowing the offensive wrestler to get inside.

INSIDE CONTROL FROM THE KNEES

Setup

W1 begins this drill on one knee with W2 behind him.

Action

Again, W1 uses tight inside control and keeps his back perpendicular to the mat (a). This drill has the same principles as the previous drill, but in this drill W2 is not allowed to lock his hands in this position. With inside control, W1 then acquires hand control, finishing by pivoting his knee and cutting through for the escape (b and c).

Coaching Point

When an escape has occurred, often the opponent momentarily relaxes. This is the time for a quick takedown maneuver.

Common Errors

It is important that the defensive wrestler not ball up as he is executing the escape so the offensive wrestler cannot cradle him in a real match situation. Balling up is a common error with this stand-up drill.

Variation

As the year progresses, W1 can add a finishing variation to the inside control drill after escaping. In the knee position, after escaping, W1 can snap W2 down and spin behind him. In the standing position, W1 can shoot a double-leg takedown on W2.

HEAVY DRILLS WHEN OPPONENT HAS INSIDE CONTROL

Setup

W2 has inside control (hands locked) in the standing position behind W1.

Action

When W2 gains inside control in the standing position, there are two techniques W1 can use to make his body "heavy" and prevent W2 from bringing W1 to the mat. The first technique involves W1 pushing W2's leg away from his body while W1 forces his own hips away (*a*). The second technique is taught when W2 is up tight against W1's body. If W2's hips are close to W1's hips, W1 locks one of his legs on the outside of W2's leg (*b*).

Coaching Points

Stress that this drill eliminates the offensive wrestler's ability to lift his opponent off the mat. It is easy to teach and very effective for stopping the offensive wrestler from bringing the defensive wrestler to the mat.

LAND LIKE A CAT

Setup

W1 is lifted off the mat with W2 behind him. W2 prepares to drive W1 to the mat to W1's side (*a*).

Action

If W1 is lifted off the mat, he must land like a cat (on hands and knees) in the proper defensive referee's position (*b*). W1 follows up with a forward-moving cat crawl to a switch or stand-up.

Coaching Point

The wrestlers need to know how important it is to quickly crawl out for the switch or stand-up before the opponent has time to adjust into a riding mode.

WHIZZER ESCAPE

Setup

W1 is in the standing position with W2 behind and hands locked around W1's waist.

Action

W1 twists around while grasping W2's hands, repositioning them on his outside hip (*a*). At this point, W1 whips his inside arm around W2's shoulder, executing the whizzer and tripping W2's inside leg backward (*b*). W1 finishes the maneuver by pushing W2's head away with his free hand, thus facing W2 for the escape (*c*).

Coaching Points

Emphasize that the whizzer should be driven with force to break the offensive wrestler's locked hands around the defensive wrestler's waist. This must immediately be followed by a quick head push away to successfully secure the escape. It is also important not to relax at this point because the offensive wrestler will have the opportunity for a second-effort takedown.

SWITCH

Setup

The wrestlers start in the referee's position (*a*) with W2 on the left side.

Action

On the whistle, W1 hits a switch, landing on his right buttock and driving his right hand between W2's legs and hip-heisting behind W2 for the reversal (*b*). Next, W2 (becoming W1) performs the switch on the whistle. This continuous (role-reversing) whistle drill lasts 15 to 30 seconds, giving each wrestler the opportunity to perform the switch.

Coaching Point

First expose the wrestlers to the hip-heist drill, as illustrated in chapter 8.

Common Error

Inexperienced wrestlers have a tendency to reach the switch arm over the top of the wrestler's back. This bad habit must be broken immediately.

SCHICKEL SWITCH

Setup

W1 is in the standing position with W2 behind and hands clamped.

Action

In this position, W1 slaps W2's leg on one side, faking a switch, and then executing a switch on the other side (*a* and *b*).

Variation

A variation of this maneuver is the suicide switch. Again, the defensive wrestler fakes a slap to one side (or both sides) of the offensive wrestler. Then the defensive wrestler drops his head toward the mat. Before the defensive wrestler's head touches the mat, he hits a hard switch. It is a very effective alternative.

RUNNING SWITCH

Setup

W1 is in the defensive starting position with W2 mounting W1 on the left side.

Action

As soon as the referee blows his whistle, W1 quickly starts running forward on all fours with his right arm and leg moving forward first (*a*), followed by W1's left arm and leg (*b*) doing the same. After performing this sequence two times, W1 executes the switch reversal (*c*).

Coaching Points

It would be wise to perform this drill as a solitary shadow-wrestling activity (detailed in chapter 8) before doing it with a partner. This will not only help the wrestlers work on their speed but also assist them in performing the maneuver in the proper sequence. Finally, should the offensive wrestler mount the bottom wrestler on the right, the defensive wrestler should start the running switch sequence with the left arm and leg.

INSIDE (OR REVERSE) SWITCH

Setup

W1 is in the defensive starting position with W2 mounting W1 on the left side.

Action

On the referee's whistle, W1 lifts up, pivoting on his left foot, and sits through his right leg toward W2, driving his left elbow into W2's rib cage (*a*). W1 finishes by going behind W2 to score the inside switch reversal (*b* and *c*).

Coaching Points

One important point to make regarding the inside switch is it should be performed *only* if the offensive wrestler has a tendency to drive into the defensive wrestler on the whistle. This is where scouting comes into play. If you observe an offensive wrestler drive into the defensive wrestler on the whistle, it's then that you teach your wrestler the inside switch.

SIT-IN TO TURN-OUT

Setup

W1 is in the defensive starting position with W2 mounting W1 on the left side.

Action

On the referee's whistle, W1 lifts up, pivoting on his left foot, and sits through his right leg forward, forcing his left elbow into W2's rib cage (*a*). W1 completes the maneuver by turning out and away from W2 (*b*).

Coaching Points

One important point to make regarding the sit-in, like the inside switch, is that it should be executed *only* if the offensive wrestler has a tendency to drive into the defensive wrestler on the whistle. This also would be learned through scouting your opponents.

SIT-OUT TURN-IN TO SWITCH

Setup

W1 is in the defensive starting position with W2 mounting W1 on the left side.

Action

On the referee's whistle, W1 sits out (*a*) and then turns in (*b*). At that point, W1 changes direction by finishing with a switch (*c*).

Coaching Points

As previously mentioned, the main purpose of this drill is to teach your wrestlers to change direction in the defensive position. Never forget that if your wrestlers only move in one direction, it is much easier for the offensive wrestlers to follow and restrain them.

SIT-OUT TURN-IN TO PETERSON ROLL

Setup

W1 is in the defensive starting position with W2 mounting W1 on the left side.

Action

This drill should be implemented after your wrestlers are exposed to the sit-out turn-in and Peterson roll tactics. On the referee's whistle, W1 sits out and then turns in as demonstrated in the previous drill. At that point, W1 forces his right leg against his left leg and tightly grabs W2's wrist (*a*). He then rolls through, using his left arm and leg to flip W2 over (*b*). He completes the move by turning toward W2's legs to gain control (*c*).

Coaching Points

This drill is very effective because as W2 follows W1's sit-out turn-in maneuver, W2 often has a tendency to be too high when he follows W1. This is the perfect time to execute the side roll. The move must be done without hesitation so W2 does not have time to readjust.

GRANBY-ROLL SERIES

Setup

The wrestlers start in the referee's position.

Action

Granby Roll for a Reversal: In the referee's position, W1 begins by posting his left hand and grabbing W2's wrist with his right hand (*a*). Next, W1 raises his hips (on his toes), making a T with his feet and tucking his chin against his chest. W1 then rolls across the tops of his shoulders, holding W2's wrist and spinning around on top of W2 for the reversal (*b* and *c*).

Granby Roll for an Escape: W1 performs the same motions for the reversal, rolling across the top of his shoulders, releasing W2's wrist, and scoring the escape (*d*).

Coaching Points

Emphasize the coaching point demonstrated in the upper-shoulder roll drill in chapter 1. Remember, each of your wrestlers must tuck his head and roll on his upper shoulders and no lower.

STAND-UP ESCAPE

Setup

W1 is in the defensive starting position with W2 mounting W1 on the left side.

Action

On the referee's whistle, W1 steps up on his left foot while driving his left elbow toward W2's chest and his right hand grabbing W2's right hand (*a*). Next, W1 comes completely to his feet, popping his hips out (*b*) and turning to the right for the escape facing W2, still grasping W2's right hand (*c*).

Coaching Points

This escape drill must be performed quickly. W1 needs to make sure he drives his left elbow into W2's chest, preventing W2's left arm from locking onto his right arm as W1 stands up. The stand-up is the safest maneuver that eliminates the opportunity for the offensive wrestler to put the defensive wrestler on his back.

Common Error

Not controlling the opponent's hands while executing the stand-up escape is a common problem.

STANDING PETERSON ROLL

Setup

W2 is behind W1 with hands locked in the standing position.

Action

In this position, W1 steps behind one of W2's legs with the arm closest to W2's body around the knee and the other arm controlling W2's opposite wrist (*a*). At this point, W1 falls back and trips W2 as W1 hits a Peterson roll, grasping W2's wrist with both hands (*b*).

Coaching Point

The wrestlers must have a firm foundation of proper shoulder position and wrist control before performing this drill.

MAINTAINING A GOOD BASE

Maintaining a good base is the second essential principle for escapes and reversals. The key is staying in good position: your head up, buttocks down, knees bent, and elbows in. A good base on the mat in the down position also requires your knees wide, back arched, and elbows at knee width. This principle cannot be overemphasized. I often tell my athletes, "If you get out of good position, the sin is not *being* there; it's *staying* there!"

104 DRILL

BASE-BUILDING

Setup
After W1 establishes a good base, W2 positions himself on top of W1 in the referee's position.

Action
On the whistle, W2 attempts to break W1 down to the mat as W1 struggles to maintain a good base. W2 should be very physical. The drill should last 15 to 30 seconds.

Coaching Point
Stress to the defensive wrestler the significance of lowering his center of gravity (or hips) when this drill is performed.

105 DRILL

BELLY-TO-BASE

Setup
W1 starts on his belly with his elbows in and palms on the mat shoulder-width apart. W2 is sitting or lying on top of W1 with all his weight.

Action
On the whistle, W1 quickly pushes up with both hands to the good base position previously described.

Coaching Point
If the defensive wrestler can perfect this skill, the offensive wrestler will not be afforded the opportunity to shoot a half nelson on either side when the defensive wrestler is on the mat.

SKATING

Setup

The wrestlers start in the referee's position.

Action

When W2 chops W1's near arm down, W1 dips down only to his elbow. W1 then skates forward with his knee and pulls with his arms to bring himself back to a good base.

Common Error

Encourage your wrestlers not to be driven to their bellies, which offers opponents the opportunity to take them to their backs. Going flat on their bellies is a common error that must be immediately addressed.

PROPER BASE SIT-OUT

Setup

In this solitary drill, each wrestler starts in the defensive referee's position, pretending that the offensive wrestler has mounted him on the left side (*a*).

Action

On the whistle, the wrestler lifts his right knee while simultaneously sitting his left leg in front of him (*b*).

Coaching Point

It is important that the wrestler not let his sit-out leg lag behind because his opponent in a match will have the opportunity to control it and stop the sit-out.

Common Error

The wrestler also must not lean too far back or forward, as is stressed in the following push-and-pull drill.

PUSH-AND-PULL FROM SIT-OUT

Setup

After W1 sits out, W2 double-underhooks W1.

Action

At this point, W2 pushes and pulls W1 forward and backward. W1's mission is to scoot forward and backward on his heels, buttocks, and hands in order to keep his upper body perpendicular to the mat.

Coaching Point

This is an outstanding drill for the defensive wrestler to perfect in order to avoid being cradled or snapped back to his shoulders.

Variation

A variation is a solitary drill in which the wrestlers scoot back and forth on their buttocks, keeping their upper body perpendicular to the mat.

ESCAPE AND REVERSAL COUNTER DRILLS

This section is divided into two general escape and reversal counter areas. Phase one stresses basic counter drills in the lifting and standing positions. In phase two, counter drills on the mat are taught.

Basic Lifting and Standing Drills

Basic lifting and standing drills assist the wrestlers in developing standing-position strategies for taking an opponent to the mat, with or without having hands locked.

109 DRILL

LIFT AND SWEEP

Setup

The wrestlers start in the neutral position, W1 behind W2 with hands locked.

Action

W1 lifts his partner in the air. With one of his knees, W1 sweeps out W2's legs (a). Then W1 brings W2 to the mat so that he lands on his side (b).

Coaching Points

The offensive wrestler must make sure his knee sweeps at the side of the defensive wrestler's thigh. As always, stress good hip positioning.

LAST-RESORT LEG TACKLE

Setup

W1 is standing behind W2, who has broken W1's hand lock and is about to escape.

Action

As a last resort, W1 lowers his hip level and double-leg tackles W2 at knee level or below.

Coaching Point

Lowering the hips and driving into the opponent with the shoulder are important in the successful execution of this drill.

Common Error

Not dropping quickly while immediately driving the opponent forward with the rear double-leg tackle is a mistake that should be corrected.

Mat Wrestling Counter Drills

The following drills demonstrate counters that offensive wrestlers can use when down on the mat. They provide the wrestlers with an arsenal of escape and reversal restraining maneuvers. Pay particular attention to hip location and the offensive wrestler's center of gravity. Hip position is essential to controlling the defensive wrestler.

SWITCH HIGH-LEG COUNTER

Setup
The wrestlers begin the drill in the referee's position.

Action
On the whistle, W2 switches to one side (a). W1 lifts the leg to the side of W2's switch. W1 lifts his leg as high as possible and floats behind W2, who fails to complete the switch (b). W1 then assumes the referee's position on the other side of W2. W2 hits a switch on the opposite side. This switching from side to side should last 15 to 30 seconds.

Coaching Point
Stress quick action and follow-through by the offensive wrestler when he is lifting his leg and maneuvering behind the defensive wrestler.

LIMP-ARM COUNTER TO SWITCH

Setup

The wrestlers start in the referee's position.

Action

W2 performs a switch. At the same time, W1 limp-arms, whipping the arm out in a circular motion (a). W1's palm should face up during the limp-arm action. After W1 performs the limp-arm and as W2 falls back, W1 drives his chest to W2's chest while simultaneously shooting a half nelson and crotch (b).

Coaching Points

The whipping action of the arm with the palm up is very important when performing this drill. This maneuver is useful when the wrestler knows his opponent usually hits a switch on the whistle.

SINGLE UNDERHOOK AND CHIN COUNTER TO SIT-OUT

Setup

The wrestlers start in the referee's position.

Action

When W2 sits out, W1 moves to the side and underhooks W2's near arm. At the same time, W1 chins W2's near shoulder, grabbing W2's chin and forcing W2's back to the mat (*a* and *b*).

Coaching Points

All action in this drill must be executed simultaneously. The wrestlers must also be taught not to twist the chin to the side when taking an opponent to his back in order to avoid being penalized for unnecessary roughness.

CRADLE COUNTER TO SIT-OUT

Setup

The wrestlers start in the referee's position.

Action

After W2 sits out, W1 simply drives his chest forward into W2's back and executes a cradle on either side (*a* and *b*). W1 then drives W2 to his back to complete the drill.

Coaching Point

Be sure that the offensive wrestler drives his chest into the defensive wrestler's back so the defensive wrestler's head is as close as possible to his knees before performing the cradle.

SPIN-AROUND COUNTER TO GRANBY ROLL

Setup

The wrestlers start in the referee's position.

Action

As W2 begins to execute the Granby roll, W1's right hand locks around W2's upper right arm (*a*). W1 then spins around in the opposite direction of W2's Granby roll, finishing behind W2 (*b* and *c*).

Coaching Points

Stress the importance of being prepared to counter a Granby roll and lock the arm quickly to follow through by reversing direction. This drill will involve a lot of practice to perfect.

HEAD-HAND POST ROLL-THROUGH COUNTER TO GRANBY ROLL

Setup

The wrestlers start in the referee's position.

Action

When W2 initiates the Granby roll, W1 posts his free hand on the mat (*a* and *b*). W1 then shadows the Granby roll, landing on his knees behind W2 (*c*).

Coaching Point

Teach the wrestlers to roll through with their heads, landing on their knees, before working on this Granby roll counter.

CONCLUSION

The preceding drills lay the foundation for developing your athletes into solid defensive and offensive wrestlers. Depending on the circumstances you face (scouting reports, minor injuries, and so on), you may need to select those drills appropriate for the situation. Furthermore, you may find it necessary to devise variations of the drills illustrated in this chapter to fit the needs of your wrestlers.

As the year progresses, combine drills to promote flow of motion in the defensive and offensive positions. A vivid example of this strategy is chain wrestling, discussed in chapter 8. The skilled wrestler must be prepared to act quickly in the defensive position, demonstrating the ability to change directions. This will keep the offensive wrestler guessing about, rather than anticipating, his opponent's next move. Likewise, the offensive wrestler must be prepared to react to any unexpected maneuver from the defensive wrestler. This can be accomplished only in a wrestling program that stresses proper drill instruction.

In chapter 6, your attention is directed to riding drills that, when properly performed, lead to pinning combinations that can culminate into the objective of wrestling: the fall.

Riding to Pinning Combinations

Ed Peery and Bruce Burnett

A TRIBUTE TO ED PEERY

Ed Peery passed away in June of 2010 at the age of 75 after a brave battle with pancreatic cancer. However, his spirit continues in the memories of thousands of former Navy wrestlers and countless others who benefited from his positive touch and influence. Personally, there is not a single day that goes by that I do not think of Ed Peery, sometimes with tears, but usually with a smile, making me feel blessed to have been one of his wrestlers, assistant coaches, and friends for over four decades.

As most wrestling fans know, Edwin Clark Peery was the third member of his family to win three NCAA titles, matching the accomplishments of his father, Rex Peery, and his older brother, Hugh Peery, while wrestling for his father at the University of Pittsburgh.

Ed was born just a few hours before his dad won his third NCAA championship while wrestling for Oklahoma State University. It was fitting that Ed was named after Rex's legendary coach at Oklahoma State, Ed Clark Gallagher. While wrestling for Pitt, Ed won 51 of 52 matches; his only loss occurred when he wrestled up a weight class.

Ed came from behind to win all three of his NCAA championship matches, displaying the grit, determination, and depth of character that typified his wrestling ability. In addition to his mental toughness, Ed was an exceptional athlete. At Shaler High School in Pennsylvania he was an excellent 100-yard dash sprinter and was the quarterback on the football team. Later in life, he excelled in racquetball and handball.

It is also well documented that Ed Peery had an outstanding career as the head wrestling coach at the United States Naval Academy. During Ed's 27 years (1961-1987) as Navy's head coach, he produced 28 All-Americans and 48 EIWA champions with an impressive dual meet record of 311-90-13. The 311 victories and 76.7 winning percentage lead all other Navy wrestling coaches as do his 8 EIWA team titles. He was the first coach at the Naval Academy to conduct a summer sports camp, another avenue where he influenced and counseled many young wrestlers.

In 1969, Ed Peery was named the NCAA Wrestling Coach of the Year. Despite leading very demanding practices, Coach Peery had a vibrant sense of humor, and he always found a way to make the sport fun, a very, very difficult goal to achieve as a mat mentor at any level. He often smiled and said, "Wrestling is a simple sport; all you need to have is a throw-down, a hold-down, and a get-out." Coach Peery knew the details of just about every aspect of wrestling known to man, and he could demonstrate them well into his 60s better than most could in their 20s.

For his wrestling and coaching accomplishments, Ed was inducted into the National Wrestling Hall of Fame in 1980, along with his brother Hugh, joining his father, Rex, who was inducted in 1976. Following his retirement as wrestling coach, Ed continued to serve the United States Naval Academy as the deputy director of physical education department for many years, eventually retiring as a full professor after 40 years of service.

More important than Ed Peery's wrestling and coaching accomplishments is the fact that during his career, he was a positive influence on countless wrestlers, midshipmen, and others whose lives he touched within and outside of the Naval Academy. His genuine smile and outgoing personality would always light up a room when he entered. I am always amazed at how often people mention what a huge impact Ed Peery had in guiding their lives.

Ed Peery was also a devout husband to Gretchen and father to their three children. Ed was always active, never one to waste time, continually seeking new challenges. He also had a life-long devotion to his church. As a civil engineer, he was a leader in the construction of the beautiful Grace Evangelical Presbyterian Church in Davidsonville, Maryland, where he also served as an elder.

Coach Ed Peery's legacy includes his dedication to wrestling and positive influence on all whose lives he changed for the better. But more important, Ed Peery's love of God, family, and country was nonpareil.

Wayne Hicks, USNA, Class of 1966
All-American wrestler under Coach Peery
Coaching colleague and friend

Riding is the ability to control the defensive wrestler while maneuvering for a pinning combination. Controlling the hips is an essential ingredient for riding the defensive wrestler effectively. If the defensive wrestler's hips are not controlled, escapes and reversals are often the result.

When the referee's whistle initiates mat or ground wrestling, the offensive wrestler's goal is to execute breakdowns that control the defensive wrestler's hips. This is accomplished by positioning the defensive wrestler's hips as low as possible.

Wrestling is a position-reflex (or reaction) activity. The wrestler must experience the feeling of the offensive position, in addition to learning offensive skills and developing reflexes for various offensive positions. Therefore, realistic resistance by the defensive wrestler is necessary for proper development of riding skills. Insist that the wrestlers take drilling activities very seriously. Drilling, when done effectively, is at least as important as full-contact wrestling, especially in the area of offensive wrestling.

RIDING DRILLS

The offensive wrestler must destroy the defensive wrestler's base and eliminate his motion. To accomplish this goal, the wrestlers must be exposed to a variety of breakdown techniques. The following drills will assist the wrestlers in becoming successful riders.

OFFENSIVE WRESTLE WEIGHT AND CHEST POSITION

Setup

The wrestlers start in the referee's position.

Action

W1 stands on his toes and clasps his hands behind his back, then places his chest on W2's upper back (*a*). W1 drives all his weight on W2 from each side, attempting to break W2's body down to the mat (*b*). This drill should last for 30 seconds on each side.

Coaching Points

Emphasize keeping the offensive wrestler's weight and strength on the defensive wrestler. The defensive wrestler must not collapse or drop to his elbows voluntarily. Furthermore, stress that the offensive wrestler should drive down and into the defensive wrestler by using his legs while staying on his feet with knees off the mat. Finally, make sure that the offensive wrestler keeps his hips higher than the defensive wrestler does. This drill is the foundation for teaching the very important spin drill.

FORWARD TRIP

Setup

W1 is standing behind W2 with hands locked.

Action

W2 establishes a slightly forward center of gravity. At this point, W1 moves his head to the side of the locked-hands grip on W2's body (*a*). W1 then steps in front of W2's leg on the side of the locked hands and head (*b*). Next, W1 sweeps W2's ankle. Finally, W1 drives into W2 as he sweeps his foot back and up, forcing W2 down to the mat (*c*).

Coaching Points

Ensure that your wrestlers assume a proper rear standing, locked-hands position. This drill takes advantage of the defensive wrestler's center of gravity when he is leaning forward.

Common Error

Some wrestlers will release the opponent in anticipation of securing a takedown. Thus, stress the importance of keeping the opponent under control until the takedown is achieved.

THREE-QUARTER NELSON

Setup

W1 mounts W2 in the offensive referee's position on the left side prepared for the starting whistle.

Action

On the whistle, W1 laces his right leg around W2's left, forcing W2's head down with his left forearm (*a*). Next, W1 slides his right arm underneath W2's chest and overlaps his left hand (*b*). Finally, W1 drives W2's head down, forcing W2 on his shoulders (*c*).

Coaching Point

This maneuver can also be performed after W2 attempts to escape or reverse W1, but hesitates on all fours.

Variation

A variation to the Three-Quarter Nelson is W1 sliding his left arm inside W2's left arm before grasping W2's head (*d*).

LEG PINCH

Setup

The wrestlers start in the referee's position.

Action

W1 traps W2's legs together at the referee's whistle (*a*). At the same time, W1 forces W2's inside arm across his chest (*b*). Finally, W1 drives W2's upper body to the mat (*c*).

Coaching Points

The leg-pinch drill is very effective when the defensive wrestler likes to stand up. Also, you must stress the importance of having the outside knee close (but not touching) the defensive wrestler's far ankle. Since bigger wrestlers have a tendency to be slower to stand up, the leg-pinch drill is an excellent maneuver for preventing such wrestlers from standing up.

Variation

Should the defensive wrestler step up quickly with his outside leg, a variation would be to pinch the defensive wrestler's inside leg and perform the leg-pinch drill with only one leg trapped.

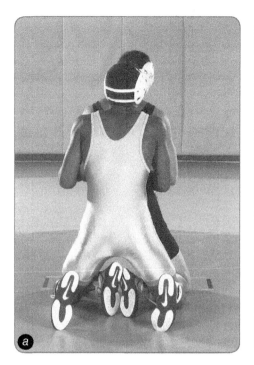

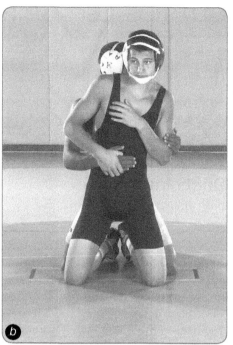

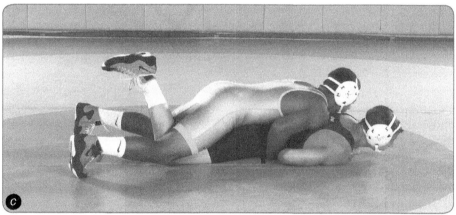

OUTSIDE LEG-UP HIP-PULL

Setup

The wrestlers start in the referee's position.

Action

W2 sits out with his outside leg up (*a*). W1 then wraps his far arm around W2's belly (*b*). W1 finishes the drill by forcing W2's near-side shoulder to the mat and stopping the escape maneuver (*c*).

Coaching Points

The offensive wrestler must press his chest into the defensive wrestler's back, forcing the defensive wrestler's chest toward his own legs while performing the drill. At the same time, the offensive wrestler breaks down the defensive wrestler's near arm to his side above the elbow to drive the defensive wrestler's inside shoulder to the mat. Thus, the offensive wrestler prevents the defensive wrestler from escaping.

INSIDE LEG-UP HIP DRIVE

Setup

The wrestlers start in the referee's position.

Action

W2 steps up on his inside leg (*a*). W1 slides his near arm across W2's belly, grabbing W2's leg from the inside with his hand while grasping W2's leg above the foot with his far hand (*b*). W1 finishes the drill by driving W2 down on his far hip (*c*).

Coaching Points

This drill maneuver must be done quickly by the offensive wrestler. Likewise, stress the need for the offensive wrestler to drive his shoulder into the defensive wrestler's near side to force him to the mat. The positioning of hands by the offensive wrestler on the defensive wrestler's far leg is also very important. Emphasize this point as the wrestlers practice the drill.

QUAD-POD STAND-UP BREAKDOWN

Setup

The wrestlers start in the referee's position.

Action

W2 lifts his body off the mat to his hands and toes (*a*). At this point, W1 wraps his right arm around W2's upper near leg, lifting it up, and slides his left hand down toward W2's near elbow (*b*). W1 finishes the drill by driving W2 down to his far shoulder and hip (*c*).

Coaching Points

When working on this drill, emphasize that the offensive wrestler lift the near leg up as high as possible with his right arm and force the defensive wrestler's near arm to his chest with his left hand. Simultaneously, the offensive wrestler must be instructed to drive across the defensive wrestler's body, forcing his far side to the mat.

TIGHT WAIST-TO-ARM BAR/ HALF NELSON

Setup

The wrestlers start in the referee's position.

Action

W1 applies pressure on W2's near arm while using a tight waist, driving W2's arm and hips to the mat (*a*). At the conclusion of the breakdown, W1 applies an arm bar (*b*). At this point, W1 jumps to the opposite side, threading the needle for a half nelson (*c*). Turning W2's back to the mat, W1 releases the arm bar to place his arm in W2's crotch (*d*).

Coaching Points

The near-arm and waist breakdown is effective for three reasons. First, it is simple to teach and execute in driving the defensive wrestler off his base. Second, it does not involve a lot of motion for the offensive wrestler, and it stresses control, driving the defensive wrestler's hips to the mat. The movement to a half nelson and crotch-pinning combination is a logical finish to the drill.

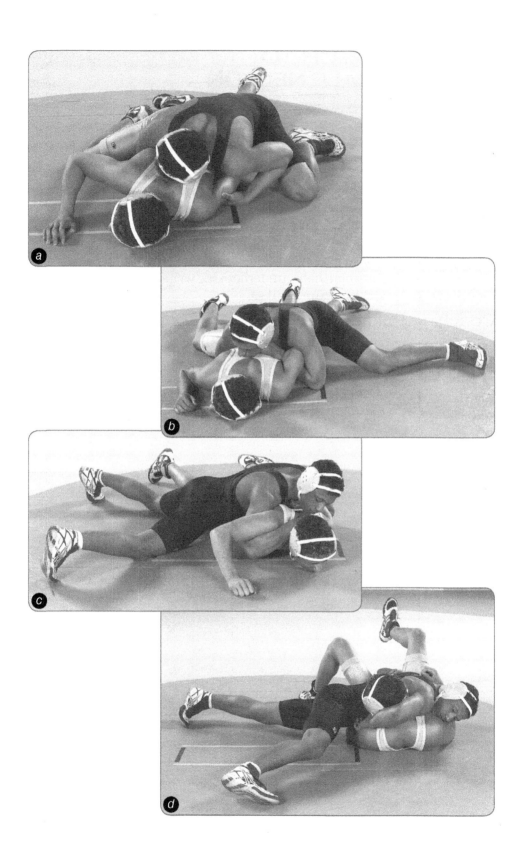

ELBOW SNATCH TO REVERSE HALF NELSON

Setup

The wrestlers start in the referee's position.

Action

W1 breaks W2 down with a tight-waist and near-elbow drive, grabbing W2's near wrist with his right hand. W1 then pinches W2's near leg with his legs while hooking W2's far elbow with his left arm (*a*). Having hooked the elbow, W1 releases W2's near wrist and then secures W2's other wrist, forcing it across his chest (*b*). W1 completes the drill by sliding his left arm around W2's head (reverse half), underhooking W2's far arm, and locking hands as he attempts to secure a fall (*c*).

Coaching Points

Wrestlers need to practice this drill on a regular basis to execute it quickly and properly. Furthermore, the offensive wrestler must pinch the defensive wrestler's near leg with his legs as tightly as possible. Note that the elbow snatch to reverse half nelson is an effective maneuver for wrestlers of all weight classes.

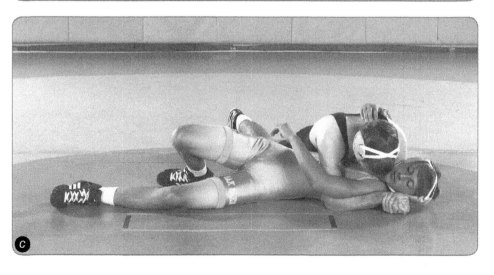

CROSSWRIST
TO CROSSFACE CHEST WRAP

Setup

The wrestlers start in the referee's position.

Action

W1 drives W2's near arm across his chest, grabbing W2's wrist with his right hand (*a*). After W1 drives W2's to the mat, W1 keeps the wrist in his grasp and reaches across W2's face, grabbing W2's far arm above the elbow (*b*). W1 finishes the drill by driving W2 to his back, still holding on to W2's wrist with his right hand (*c*).

Coaching Points

Emphasize that the offensive wrestler must drive the defensive wrestler's near shoulder to the mat as quickly as possible, placing the defensive wrestler on his belly. The crosswrist to crossface chest wrap drill can be taught to wrestlers at all levels of experience, from youth to college age.

Variation

Although this is a drill that is most suited for light- and upper-middleweight wrestlers, wrestlers in upper weight classes, including 285-pound competitors, can also perform it.

CROSSWRIST RIDE TO TURK

Setup

The wrestlers start in the referee's position.

Action

W1 drives W2's near arm across his chest, grabbing W2's wrist with his right hand and forcing W2 to the mat (*a* and *b*). W1 then lifts up W2's near leg with his left arm while stepping across W2's far leg, hooking it with his left leg (*c*). Finally, W1 drives across W2's body, using the hooked leg as a lever to force W2 to his back and finishing with the turk (*d*).

Coaching Points

It is essential that the offensive wrestler force the defensive wrestler flat on his belly before locking the far leg. At this point, the offensive wrestler must be taught to drive across the defensive wrestler's body, placing him on his back. Finally, the offensive wrestler must be instructed to finish the turk by keeping the defensive wrestler's leg locked, forcing the defensive wrestler's head to his right shoulder, and putting his free left hand on the mat to enhance body balance while working for the fall.

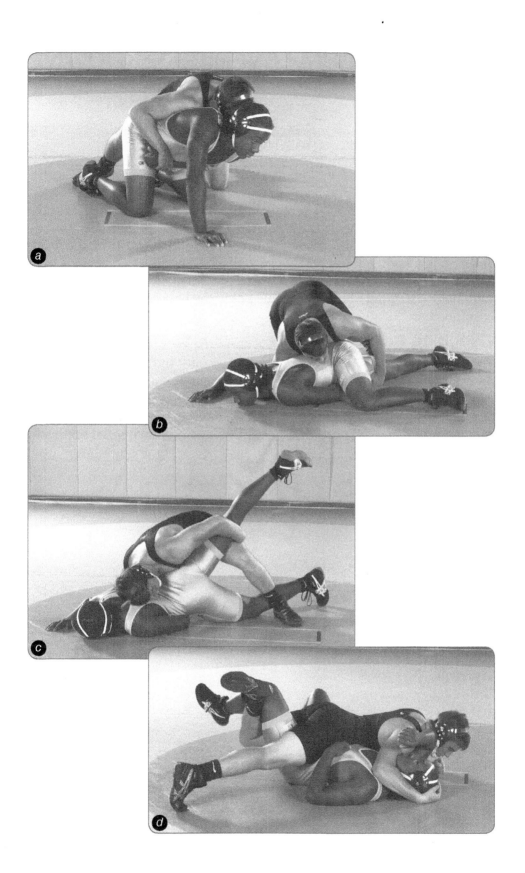

HEAD-AND-ARM LEVER BREAKDOWN TO HALF NELSON

Setup

The wrestlers start in the referee's position.

Action

W1 slides the near arm down and grasps W2's wrist while driving his head into W2's armpit (*a*). While driving W2 forward, W1 pulls W2's near wrist backward (*b*) and lifts it off the mat. When W2 is flattened on the mat, W1 can work toward the half nelson pinning combination by lifting the head-and-arm lever while forcing his head under W2's arm (*c*). Once W1's head is under W2's arm at the shoulder, great pressure can be exerted on W2's shoulder for turning him over. At this point, the half nelson maneuver can be applied on W2 (*d*).

Coaching Points

The head-and-arm lever breakdown demonstrates the fundamentals used for destroying the defensive wrestler's base. The result often is an aggressive breakdown leading to an equally dominating pinning combination. The head lever is particularly effective for beginners because it teaches a practical means of using the head as a positive force for breaking the opponent down off his base.

FAR-ARM NEAR-ANKLE BREAKDOWN TO HALF NELSON

Setup

The wrestlers start in the referee's position.

Action

W1 releases W2's near arm and reaches across W2, cupping W2's far arm above the elbow. At the same time, W1 releases the waist lock to grasp W2's near ankle (*a*). W1 accomplishes this by driving his chest into W2 and forcing him off his base to the mat (*b*). W1 then shoots the half nelson and crotch-pin hold on W2. It is important to sink the half nelson deep so that W1 has his elbow behind W2's neck (*c*).

Coaching Points

The far-arm near-ankle breakdown to half nelson demonstrates the mechanics of destroying two opposing points of the defensive wrestler's base and driving him to the mat. Some of your wrestlers may at first feel uncomfortable completely releasing an opponent's arm and waist. Point out that their chest pressure against the defensive wrestler will compensate for the momentary release.

Common Error

Maintaining chest pressure at the whistle is important for the offensive wrestler all the time: A common error when learning this drill is not maintaining chest pressure after releasing the opponent's arm and waist.

CROSSFACE CRADLE

Setup

The wrestlers start in the referee's position.

Action

W1 initiates action by releasing W2's near elbow and driving the inside of the forearm up and across W2's face, grasping the far elbow. At the same time, W1 releases the waist lock and grasps W2's far ankle (*a*). W1 must also drive the crossface to force W2's head toward his outside ankle. W1 moves the hand grasping the ankle quickly behind the back of W2's far knee (*b*). When W2's head is close to his knee, W1 locks hands for the cradle (*c*). W1 then pulls W2 back into a pinning situation (*d*).

Coaching Points

The offensive wrestler must use caution while bringing the defensive wrestler to his back. If not, the defensive wrestler can potentially kick through and end up on top in a similar situation. The point of emphasis is that once the offensive wrestler locks hands, the position becomes risky. Thus, the offensive wrestler should not rush when forcing the defensive wrestler to his back. Note: This maneuver is recommended for situations in which the pin is essential for team points or getting back into the match.

Common Error

A common mistake is quickly whipping the opponent back with the cradle rather than slowly maneuvering him to his back.

NEAR-ARM/WAIST-TO-CROSSFACE CRADLE

Setup

The wrestlers start in the referee's position.

Action

W1 breaks W2 down to the mat (*a*). After breaking W2 down, W1 watches for W2's reaction. If W2's head is low or on the mat, it isn't likely that he plans a quick reaction, so W1 can release pressure on the tight waist and near arm. From that point, W1 moves higher and forward in preparation for applying the crossface (*b*). Once his legs and feet are positioned, W1 drives the crossface across W2's face, forcing W2's head toward his outside knee (*c*). When the hands are locked, W1 completes the maneuver as previously instructed for the crossface cradle drill earlier in the chapter (*d*). Again, stress caution and deliberation when W1 brings W2 to his back.

Coaching Points

Although the concluding aspect of this drill is the same as in the crossface cradle drill, keep emphasizing proper finishing skills. Never assume anything, including knowledge of drills formerly taught.

CROSSBODY RIDE

Setup

This drill starts with W1 in the back crab-ride position.

Action

First, W1 puts a leg in while blocking W2's elbow on the same side so W2 cannot block as the leg is being applied (*a*). Next, W1 adjusts his position above and across W2's back. W1's outside arm reaches under W2's far arm. He locks hands and forces W2's head down with the inside elbow (*b*). From here, W1 drives W2 to the mat and toward his back (*c*).

Coaching Points

With repetition, most wrestlers will learn this move without difficulty. Both partners should cooperate by resisting the offensive wrestler as he forces the defensive wrestler to the mat. The crossbody ride drill is the first position that should be taught for leg wrestling. The logical progression is to move from the crossbody to the guillotine pinning combination that is discussed next.

GUILLOTINE

Setup

W1 is in the crossbody ride position with W2 on his hands and knees.

Action

Using both arms, W1 secures the trapped arm with inside grips (*a*). W1 raises W2's arm in preparation for forcing the arm overhead (*b*). Once the arm is raised overhead, W1 places the near arm around W2's neck while holding the arm at the wrist (*c*). W1 then lies back into W2's arm, creating pressure that forces W2's shoulders toward the mat. W1 creates additional pressure by wrapping his arms around W2's head in tandem with arching his back (*d*).

Coaching Points

Emphasize the importance of the offensive wrestler keeping his hips tight and high on the defensive wrestler. Allow the wrestlers to perform this drill many times during practice.

JACOB'S RIDE

Setup

The wrestlers begin the drill with W1 in the crossbody ride position (*a*).

Action

As W2 sits out with his free leg, W1 overhooks W2's near arm, placing his palm on W2's back (*b*). Simultaneously, W1 hips into W2, driving his shoulder into W2 and lifting his laced leg to the ceiling for further pressure on W2's body (*c*).

Coaching Points

Jacob's ride is an offspring of the crossbody ride drill in which the defensive wrestler sits out with his free leg. It is very important to stress proper hip and shoulder pressure on the defensive wrestler. If not, the defensive wrestler could react with a short arm drag for the reversal. The success of this drill depends on much repetition by all your wrestlers.

Common Error

A common mistake is not asserting proper pressure, which gives the defensive wrestler the opportunity to react with a short arm drag for the reversal.

Variation

A variation of the Jacob's ride drill is the crosswrist to turk drill, which is illustrated in chapter 7.

RIDING COUNTER DRILLS

Wrestling is a sport of action and reaction. The defensive wrestler must be prepared to react without hesitation to the offensive wrestler's ride techniques. This can be accomplished by having the defensive wrestler perfect the following riding counter drills.

FREEING HANDS AND WRIST

Setup

The drill starts with W2 standing behind W1, holding one arm with a two-hand grip on the wrist (a).

Action

W1 then maneuvers his free arm under W2's arm, grabbing W2's far hand (b). Next, W1 pries up, placing pressure on W2's wrist. This forces W2 to release the near-side grip on W1 (c). At this point, W1 extends the arm that W2 still controls and turns it away from the body, freeing W2's grip on the arm (d). Finally, W1 draws his elbows back to the inside position as quickly as possible in preparation for an escape or reversal maneuver.

Coaching Points

While each wrestler takes turns performing this drill, emphasize the importance of the defensive wrestler not reaching across his body, which would allow the offensive wrestler to regain wrist control. After standing up, the defensive wrestler must be concerned with keeping his hands and wrists free. There is not much the defensive wrestler can do in the standing position if his hands and wrists are controlled. In essence, the defensive wrestler must free his wrists to free his hands.

GIZONI STANDING

Setup

W1 starts in the standing position with his elbows tight against the body and W2 behind him. W2 has one arm around W1's waist and the other hand on W1's biceps. Both wrestlers' legs are bent (*a*).

Action

The drill is initiated by W1 grabbing W2's hand, which is across W1's biceps (*b*). Next, W1 raises his hand while driving his elbow back through W2's armpit (*c*). Finally, W1 backs his hips underneath the lifted arm and finishes in control (*d*).

Coaching Points

This drill is quick because once the defensive wrestler gains control, his drill partner becomes the drill wrestler, performing the same drill. Continue the drill until you want to end it. The goal is for the wrestlers to react to the situation without thinking.

GIZONI SITTING

Setup

The starting position for this drill places W1 in the sitting position. W2 has one arm around W1's waist and the other hand on W1's biceps (*a*).

Action

W1 reaches across his body and grasps W2's wrist, freeing W2's hand from the biceps (*b*). W1 places his head on the mat, performing a turn-in maneuver. At the same time, the arm that W2 controlled is raised up and under W2's armpit, reversing W2 (*c*).

Coaching Points

The major advantage of this drill is the development of a reflex action with minimum investment of effort. Like the previous drill, this drill is quick because once the defensive wrestler gains control, his drill partner becomes the drill wrestler, performing the same drill. Continue the drill until you want to end it.

SOLITARY HALF NELSON
BRIDGING COUNTER

Setup

The wrestlers start this solitary bridge drill by lying on their backs (*a*).

Action

As they bridge on their necks, instruct the wrestlers to touch both ears and roll up, touching their noses to the mat. While in the bridging position, teach the wrestlers to perform upside-down push-ups. Finally, have the wrestlers bridge as high as they can (*b*). In this position, they are to quickly drop down from the bridge, forcing their hips away from an imaginary opponent. At the same time, they are to thrust the hand and arm between his and the imaginary opponent's chest, recovering to the belly and then to a defensive referee's position base (*c* and *d*). They should practice forcing their hips to one side and then the other.

Coaching Points

This drill involves bridging, which is not typical in calisthenics. In fact, it is foreign to the majority of other sports, but in wrestling it is a must. Sooner or later all wrestlers are put to their backs. At this point, it is either bridge or get pinned. Many of the younger wrestlers may lack the neck strength for this drill. Allow them to use their hands as props while bridging. Also, you can teach these wrestlers to prop their elbows on the mat to stay off their shoulders. Above all, emphasize to the wrestlers the importance of getting off their backs.

Variation

When working with younger wrestlers, a variation is to allow them to also use their hands as further support.

HALF NELSON BRIDGING COUNTER WITH PARTNER

Setup

This drill is performed the same as the solitary half nelson bridging counter drill except now W2 is holding W1 down.

Action

W1 lies on his back, and W2 secures a tight half nelson and crotch (*a*). On the whistle, W1 hits a bridge, forcing his outside arm between his and W2's chest (*b*). Next, W1 quickly drops his back to the mat, shooting his outside arm inward while scissoring his inside leg away from W2 (*c*). The drill ends with W1 regaining a defensive referee's position base (*d*). This drill should be repeated while thrusting the outside arm inside with the half nelson and the inside arm outside with the reverse half nelson.

Coaching Points

You should first teach the drill with minimum resistance from the offensive wrestler, gradually building up to full resistance. This drill should be a part of the warm-up exercises in every practice during wrestling season. You can teach many lessons about the sport of wrestling when teaching this drill. First, the team concept is realized by not giving up a fall. Second, the individual concept of being competitive is learned by not quitting when the wrestler is on his back. Finally, the wrestlers learn to give their all and fight to the end.

140 DRILL

HALF NELSON COUNTER FROM THE REFEREE'S POSITION

Setup

This drill starts in the referee's position.

Action

W2 shoots a half nelson from the knees. W1 quickly locks his arm above the elbow of W2's half nelson arm (*a*). As soon as the arm is hooked, W1 hits a near-side roll (*b*). W1 then springs across W2's chest. Important point: W1 must spring over W2 with chest on chest (*c*). If W1 rolls his back over W2's chest, W2 will just roll through and end up on top again.

Coaching Points

Use this drill during the first days of the wrestling season. Much is learned about wrestling by learning to avoid the pin. It is difficult to stay off your back, but it is even more difficult to get off your back. Intense drills will assist in eliminating this problem.

HEAD-BEHIND-ARM COUNTER

Setup

The wrestlers start in the referee's position.

Action

As W2 attempts the head-and-arm lever, W1 drops the near elbow to the mat. At the same time, W1 points the near hand away to prevent W2 from tying up the wrist. Without W2 gaining wrist control, the head-behind-arm maneuver cannot be accomplished.

Coaching Points

This drill emphasizes that the defensive wrestler must avoid letting his wrists, hands, and arms get tied up. The base-building drill and the skating drill (chapter 5) are also helpful in achieving this wrestling skill.

142

FORWARD KNEE PINCH
CROSSBODY RIDE COUNTER

This drill and the next demonstrate how to counter the crossbody ride before it is applied.

Setup

The wrestlers start in the referee's position.

Action

The first counter drill to the crossbody ride is the forward knee pinch. Knowing that W2 will attempt the crossbody ride, W1 quickly moves the near knee forward, pinching the far leg.

Coaching Points

As in the cradle, the best defense for the crossbody ride is not allowing the top man to secure it. The scouting report will let the wrestler know in advance that his opponent uses the crossbody ride.

ARM BLOCK CROSSBODY RIDE COUNTER

The second crossbody ride counter drill is the arm block. Not only does this counter block the crossbody ride, but it also affords W1 the opportunity to reverse W2.

Setup

The wrestlers start in the referee's position.

Action

W1 pinches the near arm against his near leg as W2 attempts to apply the crossbody ride (a). Next, W1 curls his arm around W2's leg as W2 attempts the crossbody ride (b). Finally, W1 pulls W2's leg over his shoulder and head, coming out the back door and securing a reversal (c and d).

Coaching Point

Practice partners should repeat these drills many times throughout the season because the crossbody ride is a popular maneuver. By perfecting these two counters, a wrestler not only can stop the crossbody ride, but he can also eliminate the possibility of the painful guillotine.

CONCLUSION

Much can be said about riding an opponent. On occasion, I lost the standing (or takedown) phase of the match but dominated the mat or ground phase. Riding control with authority demoralizes the opposing wrestler. Such riding superiority can be accomplished only by drilling.

Drilling is absolutely essential for success in wrestling. You must incorporate drills during every warm-up session. In doing so, make drilling both an active and fun experience. Most important, the coach must be very involved during drilling sessions by directing, observing, and correcting. End every warm-up session with some full-resistance situation wrestling (detailed fully in chapter 9). Drilling in the practice room is an imperative activity. Plan it and execute it daily.

Chapter 7 offers more offensive maneuvers for the mat or ground-wrestling phase. The initial emphasis of the chapter is on those drills that prepare the wrestlers for pinning combinations, while the latter half covers advanced pinning combinations.

Advanced Pinning Combinations

Jim Akerly and Craig Turnbull

" *Great works are performed not by strength, but by perseverance.* "

Samuel Johnson

Wrestling is a sport of positioning. The wrestler who creates and maintains the better hip position is more likely to win. In the offensive position, it's a must. If a wrestler can maintain proper body position while remaining under control, the defensive wrestler will be hard-pressed to score an escape or reversal. And this is the prerequisite for working toward the ultimate goal of wrestling: the fall.

The challenge of mat wrestling for the offensive wrestler is to make the defensive wrestler's position longer, driving his hips to the mat. The top wrestler's goal is to destroy his opponent's position and attack for the fall.

Far too often, the offensive wrestler is satisfied with controlling his opponent and fails to finish with a pinning combination. The purpose of the following drills is not only to control the bottom wrestler but to follow up with pinning combinations that secure near-falls or falls.

Chapters 5 and 6 included many drills and counter drills that teach wrestlers how to avoid being pinned. Chapter 6 exposed the reader to a number of related riding to pinning drills. The emphasis of this chapter is to introduce more advanced pinning combination drills.

PREPINNING WARM-UP DRILLS

Expose your wrestlers to the following warm-up drills as a prerequisite for demonstrating various pinning techniques. Done at the beginning of practice, these warm-up drills not only prepare the wrestlers for the rest of the workout but assist in improving the execution of a number of pinning maneuvers.

MONKEY ON THE BACK

Setup

The drill begins with W2 in the referee's position. W1 assumes a chest-to-back position, underhooking W2's arms with his feet hooking W2's ankles (*a* and *b*).

Action

On the whistle, W2 rolls and drops to his elbows in the directions of his choice. W2 tries to whip W1 off while W1 tries to stay against W2's body (*c* and *d*).

Coaching Points

The purpose of this drill is to teach the offensive wrestler to ride the defensive wrestler with tight contact before executing any pinning combination. The drill should last 15 to 30 seconds before partners change positions. Three to five reps per wrestler will suffice.

TILT LOADING

Setup

W2 is in the referee's position. W1 is on his feet with knees bent, grabbing W2's far hip with both hands (*a*).

Action

W1 tilts W2 by pulling him back into his hips, keeping W2's hips on top of his hips (*b*). Once W2 is pulled back, W1 must attend to pinching his knees against W2's left leg. He must also stay perpendicular to the bottom wrestler (*c* and *d*).

Coaching Points

It is imperative to teach proper tilt positioning. Thus, the offensive wrestler must keep his inside thigh against the defensive wrestler's belly. Each practice partner should take turns performing the tilt loading drill as long as you see fit to do so.

SPIRAL BREAKDOWN

Setup

The wrestlers start in the referee's position.

Action

W1 steps to the side on his toes, wrapping his left arm deep inside W2's far shoulder (*a*). At the same time, W1 keeps his shoulder in W2's armpit, lifting his elbow and forcing W2's arm to start coming off the mat (*b*). W1 continues the move by pressuring the far hand and prying the far thigh of W2 in a circular motion (*c*).

W1 finishes the drill by securing W2's near wrist, maintaining pressure on W2's back while spinning behind (*d*). From this position, W1 considers his pinning combination options in a match.

Coaching Points

Emphasize that the offensive wrestler should stay off his knees as each partner performs the drill. Remember, drills practiced poorly or without proper technique are a waste of time.

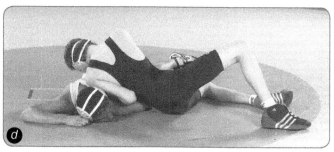

WRIST-TO-BACK

Setup

The wrestlers start in the referee's position.

Action

In this drill, W1 secures W2's near wrist, pulling it inside while pressuring his back (*a*). While constantly exerting pressure on W2's back, W1 places W2's wrist on his back in preparation for a pinning combination (*b* and *c*).

Coaching Points

The offensive wrestler must stay off the knees when applying pressure to the defensive wrestler's back. Also, should the offensive wrestler have trouble pulling the wrist out, he can reach with his free hand, grabbing the defensive wrestler's four fingers to assist in putting his arm on his back. Have both wrestlers take turns practicing this drill until you are satisfied they have executed the drill correctly.

Common Error

The offensive wrestler must not take the arm to more than a 90-degree angle to the bottom man's body, or it could become illegal. Carefully observe the drill partners as they perform this drill.

ADVANCED PINNING COMBINATION DRILLS

After the wrestlers have perfected the various breakdown and fundamental fall techniques, you can begin demonstrating higher-level pinning combination drills, such as the following. It is imperative that you devote additional time to demonstrating and observing the wrestlers performing these advanced pinning maneuvers.

148 DRILL

HIGH HALF NELSON

Setup

W2 is on his chest with W1 scissoring around the near leg. Also, W1 lifts W2's knees off the mat with forward pressure on W2 (*a*).

Action

W1 grabs W2's far wrist with his near hand. Simultaneously, W1 reaches under W2's far arm and grabs his own wrist with his far elbow under W2's far biceps (*b*). W1 then releases the grip he has on his own hand, shooting a deep half nelson. Immediately after applying the half nelson, W1 steps out to the side of the half nelson. W1 should be perpendicular to W2 as he begins to force him to his back (*c*). W1 finishes the drill with his chest on W2's, legs stretched and on his toes, pressing W2's shoulders to the mat for the pin.

Coaching Point

Although the high half nelson is considered intermediate in difficulty, finishing the drill should be stressed with novice wrestlers as well. This is another bread-and-butter maneuver that should never be overlooked in the practice room.

Common Error

A common mistake is that the offensive wrestler stays on his knees instead of keeping the pressure on by driving off his toes to force the defensive wrestler to his back.

ARM BAR AND HALF NELSON

Setup

Begin with W2 on his belly and W1 applying a far arm bar and near-side half.

Action

W1 secures an arm bar and applies a half nelson on the opposite side with the hand deep over W2's neck (*a*). W1 then pries the half nelson, forcing W2's head away from the arm bar. Loosening the arm bar slightly, W1 begins to turn W2 to his back. W1's hips must be low while he stays on his toes (*b*). The drill is completed with W1 chest to chest against W2, applying a tight half nelson and planting his toes on the mat with his head level (*c*).

Coaching Points

Stress that the offensive wrestler must loosen the arm bar as he deepens the half nelson. The arm bar and half nelson is one of the most successful pinning combinations in wrestling, so wrestlers should practice it often.

150 DRILL

ARM BAR AND HALF NELSON STACK

Setup

The drill starts with W2 on his belly and W1 applying a far half nelson and near arm bar.

Action

W1 tightens the arm bar on the near side and the half nelson on W2's far side (*a*). Next, W1 drives into W2, forcing his arm under on the half nelson side (*b*). W1 drives the side of his back into W2's back, pushing off his feet to complete the arm bar and half stack (*c*).

Coaching Points

The pressure applied by the offensive wrestler pushing off his toes is significant at the conclusion of the drill. Have partners take turns working on this drill until you are satisfied with their performance.

ARM BAR AND PEC TILT

Setup

W2 lies on his belly with his left arm in front and slightly bent. W1 has his chest on W2's back while applying an arm bar on W2 (*a*).

Action

W1 reaches his left arm across W2's face and grabs the far pectoral area. W1 then drives W2's far shoulder toward his ear and jams the near knee under W2's near hip, tilting him into a near-fall position (*b*). W1 finishes the drill by hipping into W2 as his right leg reaches across W2's thigh. W1 also locks his right leg so W2 cannot bridge effectively (*c*).

Coaching Point

The offensive wrestler's hip positioning is very important, so guide the drill partners slowly at first for proper technique. Speed can increase with practice.

Common Error

Improper hip positioning is a common error when practicing this drill.

DRILL

CROSSWRIST TO TURK

Setup

The wrestlers start in the referee's position with W1 in a basic two-on-one arm ride on W2's left arm.

Action

W1 drives W2's belly to the mat, executing a crossface with his left arm while still controlling W2's left wrist with his right hand (*a*). Next, W1 quickly releases W2's wrist just before reaching for W2's near leg (*b*). At the same time, W1 keeps body pressure on W2 by driving off his feet into W2. Continuing the drill, W1 picks up W2's near leg at the knee with his right hand while wrapping his right leg around W2's far leg (*c*). W1 finishes the maneuver by driving across W2, placing him on his back. He also lifts W2's head off the mat with his left hand and posts his right hand on the mat to maintain balance when completing the turk ride (*d*).

Coaching Points

Make sure that the offensive wrestler drives off his feet to keep the pressure on the defensive wrestler before lifting the defensive wrestler's near leg. The wrestlers will have to spend some time perfecting this drill under the supervision of the coaches. This drill will likely take more time than usual to perfect.

TWO-ON-ONE TILT

Setup

The wrestlers start in the referee's position.

Action

W1 secures W2's near wrist with his left hand while placing his left thigh under W2's belly. At the same time, W1 puts his right thigh against W2's near-side buttock (*a*). W1 then drives W2 to his near shoulder, staying tightly against him. Also, W1 reaches across W2's belly, grabbing W2's left wrist with his right hand. While in this two-on-one position, W1 pulls W2 to his back (*b*). W1 completes the drill with his body perpendicular to W2 and under W2's body. W1 also pinches W2's thigh with his knees, keeping his feet close to his buttocks (*c*). To avoid a defensive fall, W1 must constantly be aware of his shoulder position.

Coaching Point

Proper technique is an important factor when performing this pinning combination drill, so observe the wrestlers carefully. Do not permit a wrestler to perform this move in competition until he has perfected it to your satisfaction.

Common Errors

Hand control and proper positioning of the hips are important. Likewise, the offensive wrestler must be careful not to place his shoulders on the mat, or a defensive fall could occur. These are common errors, *especially the drill wrestler leaning on his back,* and must be eliminated.

ADVANCED PINNING DRILLS FROM A SPIRAL BREAKDOWN

After perfecting the spiral breakdown (previously discussed in the chapter) through proper drill work during practice, the wrestlers can then be introduced to the okey bar series.

OKEY BAR TO A HALF NELSON

Setup
W1 has broken W2 down from the referee's position with a spiral breakdown and posted W2's near arm across his back.

Action
While maintaining two-on-one control of W2's arm, W1 drives W2's arm across his back at an angle towards W2's far hip, keeping W2's arm close to his back (a). As W2's near shoulder comes up off of the mat, W1 drops his top shoulder below W2's near shoulder (b). As he continues to drive W2's arm towards his far hip, W1 gives up his two-on-one control. W1 then applies a half nelson with his top arm and continues to drive W2 to his back. As W2 turns to his back, W1 can release the okey bar and slide his bottom arm to an underhook position (c) to prevent W2 from turning out of the pinning combination.

Coaching Points
W1 must remain perpendicular to W2 after securing the okey bar. W1 must allow W2's controlled wrist to rotate so that his near shoulder can come away from the mat. Maintaining pressure on W2's back while driving his arm to his far hip is an important aspect to successful completion of this pinning combination.

Common Error
Not keeping pressure on the defensive wrestler's back is a common mistake.

OKEY BAR TO A CLAW

Setup

W1 has broken W2 down from the referee's position with a spiral breakdown and posted W2's near arm across his back.

Action

While maintaining two-on-one control of W2's arm, W1 drives W2's arm across his back at an angle towards W2's far hip, keeping W2's arm close to his back. In this instance, W2 turns his shoulder down, his head away, and posts his far arm (*a*). While maintaining pressure, W1 hops across W2's body and drives his bottom arm under W2's armpit to a claw position (*b*). W1 must anchor his palm on the far side of W2's neck. W1 uses this position to drive W2 over his posted shoulder to his back. W1 can let his claw become a reverse half (*c*), or he can change it to a regular half nelson.

Common Error

W1 must maintain pressure as he hops across. Not doing so is a common error that must be carefully observed by the coach. He should continue to control W2's arm, even after W2 has been turned to his back, and stay perpendicular to W2 while attempting to secure the fall.

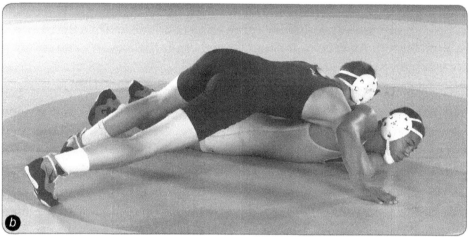

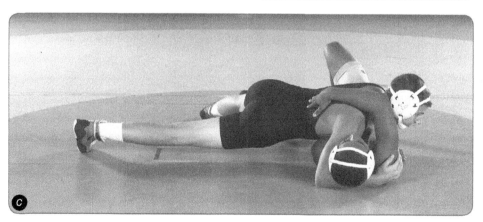

OKEY BAR TO A TURK
WITH A CROSSFACE

Setup

W1 has broken W2 down from the referee's position with a spiral breakdown and posted W2's near arm across his back.

Action

In this situation W2 keeps his near shoulder down and has his head turned away from W1. W2's far arm is kept close to his body, preventing W1 from hopping across and securing the claw (*a*). W1 releases his two-on-one control on the okey bar and lifts W2's near hip by picking up W2's near knee with his low arm. As space is created, W1 then steps under W2's near leg and over his far leg to secure a turk ride position (*b*). Once the turk is secured, W1 can return to the two-on-one control and continue to drive the okey bar to W2's far hip. As W2's near shoulder comes off the mat, W1 can secure a crossface to take W2 to his back (*c*).

Coaching Points

W1 must secure the turk ride by stepping over W2's far knee and staying above the knee for an effective turk ride position. As W1 turns W2, remind W1 to circle the turk towards W2's head to keep pressure and to maintain a perpendicular position through the pinning combination.

OKEY BAR TO AN ARM BAR

Setup

W1 has broken W2 down from the referee's position with a spiral breakdown and posted W2's near arm across his back.

Action

W1 continues to post W2's trapped arm to his far hip, which will get W2 to shift his weight to his attacked side. W1 should relax his pressure on W2's upper body and shift his weight across W2's hips (*a*). This will create space that will allow W1 to release his two-on-one control with his top arm and put an arm bar on W2's controlled arm (*b*). After the arm bar is secured, W1 should release W2's wrist and take control of W2's far wrist. With W2's far wrist trapped, W1 can move his weight to the arm bar side (*c*) and apply pressure on W2's shoulder by walking around W2's head and driving W2 to his back (*d*).

Coaching Points

W1 must keep constant pressure on W2's upper body after securing the arm bar. As W1 walks the arm bar over W2's head, he needs to literally put W2's shoulder in his ear. Finally, W1 should never cut the corner when walking the arm bar around W2's head. If W1 cuts the corner, the necessary pressure would be lost, allowing W2 to rise and potentially toss W1 to his back.

Common Error

The lack of body pressure by the offensive wrestler during this drill is a common error. Be particularly vigilant about spotting this error.

OKEY BAR TO A KEY LOCK

Setup

W1 has broken W2 down from the referee's position with a spiral breakdown and posted W2's near arm across his back.

Action

W2 defends W1's attempt to post his controlled arm by remaining flat on the mat (*a*). W1 then circles W2's head and threads his near hand under W2's elbow, locking on W2's controlled wrist (*b*). W1 then continues to circle to that side (*c*), releasing his control of W2's arm with his far arm. He then secures a half nelson and drives W2 to his back (*d*).

Coaching Points

W1 needs to continue to keep pressure on W2 by staying on his toes when he circles W2's head. In the finish position, W1 needs to stay perpendicular and maintain chest-on-chest pressure.

Common Errors

Again, failure to maintain proper body pressure or stay on the toes are common errors that must be caught early. By keeping W2's controlled wrist in his lower back, W1 can prevent the key lock from becoming potentially dangerous.

CONCLUSION

The main objective for every wrestler should be to score a pin or fall. However, sometimes pinning combination skills are not developed thoroughly in the mat sport. Too many wrestlers devote less time drilling in the offensive position than they devote to takedown skills. Thus, it is the responsibility of the coach to devote the appropriate amount of practice time to pinning combinations.

From a developmental perspective, creating the attitude and skills associated with scoring from the top position early in a wrestler's training will increase his ability to control his opponent and score pins. Strong skills from the offensive position will not only physically wear down the wrestler's opponent but will ultimately lead to more pins during a wrestler's career. In successful wrestling programs, winners are also pinners.

Conditioning is another important aspect of successful wrestling. Any wrestler can perfect moves through drill work, but if he is not well conditioned, failure on the mat is a distinct possibility. Chapter 8 introduces effective conditioning drills. Coaches need to place as much emphasis on conditioning as they do on wrestling skill development. After all, how often have you seen skilled wrestlers defeated by less-skilled opponents who were in better shape? The conditioning drills offered in chapter 8 will prepare wrestlers for the physical and mental aspects of the sport that are essential for lasting success on the mats.

Conditioning

Ken L. Taylor

"
Depend on the rabbit's foot if you will, but remember, it didn't work for the rabbit.
"

R.E. Shay

The purpose of conditioning skills is to supplement (not replace) wrestling. All conditioning drills should be developed with the objective of having maximum carryover to the sport itself. This is called *specificity of exercise*. Your goal is to make each conditioning drill as specific to wrestling as possible.

Fortunately, this is not difficult because wrestling requires so many levels of fitness: strength, quickness, agility, endurance, flexibility, balance, and mental toughness. Wrestling is considered by many to be the most strenuous and physically demanding sport of all, so just about any conditioning drill will have benefits for the wrestlers.

The use of conditioning drills for wrestling can accomplish the following objectives:

- **Improved strength.** Conditioning is used to increase strength in the off-season and maintain strength during the season.
- **Increased agility and quickness.** Developing these skills helps the wrestler control his body in different positions and be quicker on his feet and on the mat.
- **Enhanced endurance.** Wrestlers with developed cardiorespiratory endurance have strong finishes in matches, are able to recover more quickly, and can handle the rigors of a strenuous season.
- **Training variety.** Conditioning drills are just different enough from technique drills to alleviate tedium and keep wrestlers interested in practice.
- **Mental benefits.** Good conditioning promotes mental toughness and improves confidence.

STRENGTH DRILLS

The four major benefits of an effective strength program for wrestling are as follows:

1. When you concentrate on wrestling muscles in your strength program, the wrestlers will improve.
2. A stronger athlete is less prone to injury and will recover from injury more quickly.
3. A stronger, well-conditioned athlete can hold up to the rigors of a tough season.
4. A stronger wrestler is a more confident wrestler. He feels more able to compete and doesn't feel the misguided need to cut an inordinate amount of weight.

The first and most important goal of strength development for wrestling is *core strength*. The *core* refers to the stabilizing muscles in the center of the body, which include the hips, torso, and lower back. Think of the body as a series of electrical pathways with your midsection a sponge. You must have a good electrical conductor to carry the current. Without a conductor (water), the electrical current will not travel. The water represents a well-developed core. The stronger the core, the more efficiently energy can be transferred without being lost in the sponge.

Second, wrestling necessitates a lot of driving with the legs and pulling with the arms, so strength conditioning should address those actions. Third, wrestling is one of the few sports where neck strength is very, very important. Fourth, wrestlers need endurance strength to remain strong throughout the entire match, especially if a tie occurs, and further wrestling is required.

Finally, lifting should integrate different muscle groups at the same time. Wrestling takes place on a three-dimensional plane: up and down, left and right, and forward and backward. So strength training should involve movement in all directions.

In the exercises that follow, you will see many balancing and lifting exercises that involve movement from one plane to another. These exercises are designed to bring many different muscles into play at the same time. This promotes not only strength in isolated muscles but also increases in balance, flexibility, speed, and agility.

We want to create more powerful wrestlers. By definition, power is the product of force and speed. Power is definitely one thing we hope to gain in a good strength and conditioning program.

It is generally believed that strength gains are better accomplished through heavier weight and fewer reps (several sets of 4 to 8 reps), whereas muscular endurance is achieved with a combination of lower weight and higher reps (sets of 10 to 15 reps or more). I am not a big fan of high-weight, low-rep lifting unless athletes are properly taught, supervised, and spotted. With heavy lifting, the potential for serious injury increases, as does the tendency for athletes to "cheat" or use improper form. The last thing any wrestling coach wants is for one of his wrestlers to be injured in the weight room, especially during the season. In-season lifting should focus on endurance lifting, except for a select few wrestlers who are trying to gain weight.

In-Season Lifting Program

There is a place for lifting during the wrestling season. However, one should not lift just for the sake of lifting. Lifting activities must be organized in such a manner that the muscle groups worked are those used in wrestling. If not, the lifting program will be ineffective.

Big 10

The big 10 is a group of buddy-lifting exercises we do once a week during the season at the conclusion of practice. These exercises help with strength and endurance and enhance all the major muscle groups used in wrestling.

Keep these guidelines in mind when doing these lifting exercises:

- Each wrestler needs a buddy who is about the same weight. Heavyweights may need to lift a lighter person (coach or extra person).
- Do one lift at a time with each partner, alternating lifters, and keeping the team together.
- As the wrestlers get in better shape during the season, gradually increase the reps and distances involved.

The Big 10 approach is a very effective use of practice time. Following is a list of the 10 exercises that make up the Big 10:

Piggyback Carry

One partner carries the other piggyback style around the mat once or twice. Switch partners for each carry. This activity develops leg, arm, and back strength.

Belly-to-Back Carry

With the belly-to-back carry, the partners go only about one-half the distance as the piggyback carry. This exercise assists the participants in proper lifting techniques and strengthens the back muscles.

Buddy-on-Back Squat

One partner is in the piggyback position as the drill partner squats for 10 to 15 reps while facing close to the wall. Emphasize deep squats. This conditioning drill strengthens the legs.

Reverse Body Lifts

The drill partner in the standing position initiates the drill by facing opposite his partner with arms around the back of the body and hands locked in front (*a*). At this point, the drill partner lifts his partner off his feet from side to side (*b*). The reverse body lifts concludes after 8 to 10 lifts for each drill partner (*c*). This drill develops arm, chest, and back strength and proper lifting skills.

Handstand Push-Up

The drill partner does push-ups while his partner holds his feet in the air, standing behind (*a* and *b*). Each partner should perform 8 to 10 reps. This conditioning activity develops arm and chest strength in various body positions.

Pull-Up

The drill partner lies on his back with his partner standing and straddling him while each partner grasps the other's wrists (*a*). The drill partner then pulls himself up (*b*). Each practice partner executes 15 to 20 reps. This drill increases grip strength as well as arm and pectoral strength.

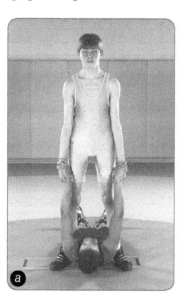

Head-Between-Legs Lift

The drill partner is positioned on all fours with his head between his partner's legs. His partner lies over the drill partner's back (*a*). The drill partner then lifts his partner off the mat (*b*). Each partner performs 6 to 10 reps. This drill strengthens the back muscles for lifting.

Four-Way Neck Exercises

The drill partner is positioned on all fours with his partner behind him. The partner then forces the drill partner's neck in different directions: down (*a*), up (*b*), and from side to side (*c*). The drill partner should give moderate neck resistance. Both partners perform six to eight reps in each direction.

Abdominal Drill

The standing partner throws the drilling partner's legs toward the mat, straight down to the left and right (*a* and *b*). Each wrestler should do 20 to 30 reps. This activity develops the abdominal muscles as the drilling partner brings his legs back up.

Fingertip Push-Up

Have your athletes do 40 to 80 reps of push-ups on their fingertips. Push-ups develop the arm and chest muscles.

Weight-Room Lifting

Do a weightlifting circuit with very little rest (10 to 15 seconds) between each lift, lifting for 20 to 30 seconds. If you use partners, one must immediately follow his partner and then rush to the next station. This program can be performed two days a week.

The alternate-day program is designed for three sets of six reps, but you might consider starting with just one or two sets so the wrestlers won't be too sore. Using eight stations, the partners should rotate from station to station. (Note: When using free weights, it's up to you to determine the appropriate weight for each wrestler.)

Day 1

Station 1: Front Squat

The wrestler holds the barbell in front, resting on his shoulders, and does full squats, developing leg and back strength.

Station 2: Standing Cable Pull

The wrestler does one set of 10 reps with one leg forward to simulate a single-leg pull-in, increasing grip and arm strength. Alternate the forward leg. Legs should be slightly bent.

Station 3: Pillar Bridge Front

The wrestler is on his knees and elbows. He raises his right arm and left leg and then the left arm and right leg. This drill strengthens the hips and buttocks.

Station 4: Towel Pull-Up

The wrestler wraps two towels around the pull-up bar before performing the pull-up activity. This promotes grip, arm, and chest strength.

Station 5: Four-Way Neck Exercise

Follow the same procedures as for the four-way neck exercises described earlier in chapter 8. Note: The number of repetitions would be the same.

Station 6: Upper-Body Twist

Holding a free weight, the wrestler moves from side to side on a physioball. This activity promotes flexibility and strength in the back muscles, as well as improved arm and grip strength.

Station 7: Abdominal Crunch

Holding a free weight, the wrestler straightens and bends his hips backward and forward (similar to a sit-up) on the physioball. This exercise increases grip, arm, and abdominal strength.

Station 8: Leg Curl

This exercise is performed on the leg machine, straightening (*a*) and bending (*b*) at the knees. This strengthens the hamstrings, calves, and thighs.

Day 2

Station 1: Dumbbell Single-Leg Squat

With one foot on the bench and the other on the floor, the wrestler holds dumbbells while dipping and raising his body. This improves leg strength and flexibility.

Station 2: Dumbbell Single-Leg RDL

Holding dumbbells, the wrestler bends forward, lifting the left leg, then returns to the upright position. He then repeats the exercise with the right leg. This strengthens the hip muscles and promotes flexibility and grip strength.

Station 3: Dumbbell Alternating Arm Press

Using the incline bench in the sitting position, the wrestler lifts the right dumbbell to the ceiling and brings it back down to the starting position, then repeats the exercise with the left arm. This activity, like push-ups, strengthens the triceps and chest muscles.

Station 4: Physioball Push-Up

The wrestler does push-ups with hands and feet on physioballs. This is not only a strength drill but also promotes body balance.

Station 5: Reverse Hyperextension

The wrestler lies with his belly on the physioball and then lifts his legs as high as he can, posting his hands. This drill is effective for hip strength and flexibility.

Station 6: High Pull

Standing with a barbell held at knee level (*a*), the wrestler lifts the barbell to his chest (*b*). This activity strengthens the back and arms.

Station 7: Back Hyperextension

Lying on his belly on a bench and holding a weight (*a*), the wrestler bends his torso down and back up (*b*). This strengthens the back.

Station 8: Dumbbell Alternating Arm Curl

The wrestler performs hammer curls, one arm at a time. Make sure palms are facing in. This weightlifting exercise increases biceps strength.

As midseason approaches, mat time is at a premium, so you may want to use high-intensity weight circuit training only once a week. You can effectively do this by combining lifts from day 1 and day 2 into a single circuit.

If you really want to get your athletes' heart rates up and keep them up, have only one wrestler at each station, letting them rest only during the 10- to 15-second interval between each station.

If you have a large number of stations, a good idea is to alternate your stations between upper-body and lower-body lifts as the wrestlers move from station to station. This promotes overall body strength and conditioning without overtaxing one part of the body. You don't want your wrestlers so exhausted during the circuit that they have to quit on their lifts. Also, with your help, the wrestlers should use the proper amount of weight to be able to really push themselves, but not so much that they cannot complete the lifts.

I encourage my wrestlers not to rest while lifting. If they must rest, they should catch their breath while their bodies are still being stressed. For example, if they are doing pull-ups, they should rest while still hanging from the bar, rather than quit by dropping to the floor. Rest while lifting weights should occur when the weight is in the air, not on the ground!

Kettlebell Drills

Kettlebells offer another form of lifting that has received a lot of attention recently. You can acquire kettlebells in various weights ranging from 5 pounds to 100 pounds. (Some brands of kettlebells are also available in metric units.) Many wrestling coaches perceive kettlebells as being more versatile in some respects than traditional dumbbells. You can grab them with either one hand or two, depending on the exercise. Following are six of the most popular lifts. They can be done in sets of the same exercise or as a circuit, going from one exercise to the next.

Warm-up: Hang a light kettlebell from each arm at your side. Twist your hands in a clockwise direction and then reverse directions. You can also take a light kettlebell and rotate it around your body, changing hands as you swing the kettlebell around your back. Rotate in each direction.

Double-Arm Swing

Stand with legs wider than shoulder-width apart with the kettlebell between the legs. With both hands, grab the kettlebell in a squat position (*a*). Then swing the kettlebell forward to the height of the shoulders (*b*). Keep the arms extended and use the power of your legs, hips, and lower back to propel the kettlebell. Once it is at shoulder height, allow the weight to descend downward between the legs; then repeat the exercise. Do 8 to 15 repetitions.

Single-Arm Swing

The swing is similar to the double-arm swing, except that the wrestler is using one arm at a time. This will force the body to use more rotation of the torso. Starting with the right arm, place the kettlebell between the legs but closer to the right leg (*a*). Then swing the kettlebell upward above the head (*b*). Finally, drop the weight back to the starting position. Do 8 to 15 repetitions with the right arm. Then repeat the procedure with the left arm.

Military Press

To do military presses with the kettlebells, wrestlers need to learn how to cradle the kettlebell in each hand without smashing or bruising the forearms. You start the exercise in the squat position, holding a kettlebell in each hand (*a*). Using a curling and cleaning motion, lift the kettlebells to shoulder height (*b*). This will involve some practice. Finally, press the kettlebells overhead (*c*). Wrestlers can either press both kettlebells at the same time or alternate arms.

Squat

Cradle the kettlebells in each hand at shoulder height. Then do conventional parallel squats. Do 15 to 20 squats using lighter-weight kettlebells.

Forward Lunge

The kettlebells are held at shoulder height. When performing the forward lunge, make sure to take a long step. The lead leg should form a 90-degree angle at the knee. Furthermore, the trailing leg should almost touch the mat. Wrestlers can lunge in place or alternate legs for 8 to 15 repetitions. Another variation would be to forward lunge 20 to 50 feet across the mat, alternating legs.

Lawn Mower

The lawn mower drill can be done bending at the waist (*a*), or by placing one hand and knee on a bench or box (*b*), lifting the kettlebell with one arm as though starting a lawn mower. Do 8 to 15 repetitions with each arm. This is a great exercise for the shoulders, and upper and lower back.

Off-Season Lifting Program

During the off-season, each of the in-season lifts can be performed with additional lifts as needed. Off-season lifting can take place three or four days a week. Wrestlers may lift three or four sets, increase the weight appropriately, and dramatically increase the time spent lifting.

The following are additional lifts and exercises that can also be a part of any weight-training program during the wrestling season:

Hang Clean

The hang clean and power clean are two of my favorite lifts. It is usually better to teach the athletes how to hang clean first. The wrestler brings the barbell from his hips to his shoulders with palms facing his body (*a* and *b*). This activity strengthens the arms, legs, and back.

Power Clean

The wrestler performs the power clean in the same manner as the hang clean, except the lift is started from the floor. This strengthening exercise is also beneficial for the legs, arms, and back.

Flat Bench Press

You can use either a straight bar or dumbbells, lifting both arms at the same time or alternating arm presses. This exercise also assists in developing the triceps.

Good Morning Squat–Jerk Complex

This is a series of athletic lifts performed in succession from the standing position. The barbell is initially on the shoulders with the body bent forward and legs straight (*a*). At this point, the wrestler squats and jerks the barbell over his head (*b* and *c*). These exercises strengthen the back, arms, and legs.

Wide-Hand Snatch

This exercise is executed in a single motion, lifting the barbell from the floor to overhead. The knees are initially bent (*a*). When lifting, the wrestler shifts his body under the barbell (*b*). The exercise finishes with legs and arms straight and the barbell over the head (*c*). This activity is beneficial for strengthening the arm, leg, and back muscles.

Dumbbell One-Arm Snatch

This exercise is executed in a single motion, with the wrestler lifting one dumbbell with one hand from the floor to over his head (*a* and *b*). The wrestler alternates the lifting arm on each repetition during this activity. This exercise develops the legs, arms, and back.

Rope Climbing

This is one of my favorite exercises for wrestling, especially using arms only. There is no better activity for arm and grip strength. Always have spotters during this activity as a safety precaution.

Lunge Across the Mat

This is another outstanding strength exercise for wrestling. It can be done by holding dumbbells at one's sides or by holding them on the shoulders (*a*). It is important that the wrestler take a deep stride on each step, lifting his knee high (*b*). This drill develops arm, leg, and back strength.

Pull-In From Push-Up Position

In the push-up position, the wrestler lifts the dumbbell toward his shoulder and side with one arm. The wrestler commonly alternates arms after 10 reps. This activity increases arm strength and improves balance.

Chin-Up Bar Pull-In

The wrestler holds the chin-up bar with hands together and palms facing opposite directions. He then attempts to lift his belly up to the bar. Use a spotter. This exercise promotes grip, arm, and abdominal strength.

CARDIOVASCULAR DRILLS

Except for wrestling, there is no substitute for running to develop cardio-vascular fitness or efficiency. Wrestlers gain many benefits from running, such as the following:

1. Running promotes cardiovascular endurance.

2. Running, especially hill running, increases strength in the legs and hips.

3. Running burns more calories in less time than just about any other activity.

4. Running is an outstanding off-season activity. It would be wise to encourage your wrestlers to compete in cross-country and other run-ning-oriented sports.

5. Running is a great way to get some sunshine and fresh air.

We strongly encourage our wrestlers to run on Sundays and on their days off. This helps to eliminate soreness in the body and rejuvenates one's energy level. The distance can vary from two to four miles or more—whatever is comfortable for each individual wrestler. We believe that Sunday runs lead to better results during the week.

Running and Related Activities During Practice

We have the wrestlers run at different times throughout practice. Note that wrestlers can wear wrestling shoes when running on the mat but should wear running shoes everywhere else. The following are ideas for practice running and related activities:

1. Before stretching at the beginning of practice, the wrestlers can run for 5 to 10 minutes, starting slowly and gradually picking up the pace. Related running activities include skipping, high-knee running, sideways run-ning, and leap running. Be creative and make it fun.

2. The wrestlers can run between teaching sessions or in preparation for live wrestling during practice.

3. Fartlek training, a jogging and sprinting activity, should be introduced midseason. Wrestling is a sport of both endurance and interval activ-ity. Fartlek running helps your wrestlers adapt to this kind of action. A rule of thumb for fartlek training is to sprint for 30 seconds and rest 30 seconds. Fartlek training should be done for 6 to 12 minutes.

4. Stair running is great for leg strength because it is more strenuous than traditional running.

5. The stationary bike is a great alternative to running. It is especially effec-tive for wrestlers with knee or ankle problems. But note that wrestlers

will have to work twice as long on stationary bikes to work off the same number of calories as running.

6. The rowing machine is also a fantastic alternative to running and biking. Works your legs and your core muscles with no impact, and only a short length of time on the machine reaps big benefits in muscle strength and cardiovascular endurance.

Cardiovascular Drills for Concluding Practice

At the end of practice, the following activities can be used.

Rope Skipping

This is a fantastic activity for promoting quickness and lightness on the feet. It assists with balance and coordination and can be an excellent workout in itself. I highly recommend Buddy Lee's books and videos on rope skipping. Buddy is an unbelievable performer and rope skipper, and his ropes are ultra fast. See www.buddyleejumpropes.com.

LOBO Round-Up

Another unique and creative activity for the conclusion of practice is the LOBO round-up. We perform the LOBO round-up every so often as a motivating, change-of-pace activity. The wrestlers really like it. Here are the particulars of the drill:

1. Turn on the music nice and loud. Coaches, choose the music, or your wrestlers will play something you hate!

2. The wrestlers work in pairs with partners of approximately the same weight.

3. Divide the wrestlers as evenly as possible into six groups for station drills.

4. Get 10-pound (5 kg) plates from the weight room for station 3, the number equal to the number of wrestlers in the largest group.

5. Place one group at each of the six stations.

6. On the whistle, the wrestlers begin the activity at their station. The drill at each station should last 20 to 30 seconds. At each station, each partner does two alternating intervals. On the coach's whistle, the groups move to the next station. The interval of time to move to the next station should be no longer than 15 seconds before starting the next activity. The stations are as follows:

Station 1

Partner A sprints across the room and back while partner B rests. Then partner B sprints while partner A rests. (Remember, the partners in each group do two intervals at each station.)

Station 2

Partner A does the designated number of push-ups with his legs propped on partner B's back, then the partners reverse roles.

Station 3

Partner A lunges forward while holding the 10-pound (5 kg) weight in front of him, keeping his arms extended. He alternates between stepping the left leg and then right leg forward (*a*). At the same time, partner B does squats while holding the 10-pound plate over his head. He must do full squats, so the thighs come down parallel to the floor (*b*). The partners then switch 10-pound plate drills.

Station 4

Partner A does the designated number of abdominal crunches while partner B holds his legs down on the mat. They then reverse positions.

Station 5

Partner A performs "ski" jumps across partner B's back. At this station, one partner is on his elbows and knees while the other stands beside him, facing the same direction and alternately jumping from side to side. They then rotate positions.

Station 6

Partner A jumps vertically as many times as he can during the time frame determined by the coach. He must jump as high as he can, lifting his knees as high as possible (a). At the same time, partner B performs a wall sit with his back against the wall and upper thighs parallel to the floor (b). He stays in that position as long as partner A vertically jumps. They then change positions.

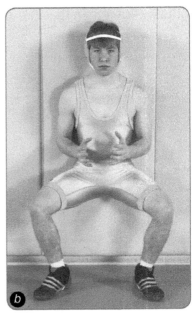

AGILITY AND QUICKNESS DRILLS

Position, technique, agility, and quickness are vital in wrestling. We must teach our wrestlers to set up their moves by creating motion, maneuvering the opponent out of position, and striking when the opponent is off-balance or out of sync.

Even counter moves are best executed by the wrestler positioning himself in a way that stymies his opposition, taking advantage of his weaknesses, and ultimately scoring.

The following activities will assist the wrestlers in developing instincts that will promote proper motion, good timing and body positioning, and agility and quickness.

SHADOW WRESTLING FROM THE NEUTRAL POSITION

Performed at the beginning of practice, shadow wrestling is a solitary activity that allows each wrestler to focus on motion, body position, and timing. We use shadow wrestling at the end of practice to work on endurance. Start very slowly and gradually increase speed. Make sure every part of the wrestlers' bodies is where it should be.

Setup

Shadow wrestling is initiated from the neutral position.

Action

The participants shadow wrestle various takedowns, increasing speed as they loosen up. This is a great way to work on defense: proper body position, protecting legs, and reacting. It should be composed of three or four periods of 30 seconds, doing as many moves as possible to promote endurance.

Coaching Points

Shadow wrestling improves quickness because it takes away an opponent's resistance, allowing the wrestler to move freely. Emphasize this during the drill. Make sure the wrestlers focus on stance, level change (hip positioning), penetration, and finishes. Always watch for common errors as they shadow wrestle in the neutral position.

SHADOW WRESTLING FROM THE BOTTOM REFEREE'S POSITION

Setup

Shadow wrestling initiates from the bottom referee's position.

Action

The wrestlers should concentrate on creating motion, getting the hips moving correctly, and exploding off the bottom. The wrestlers usually perform three or four periods of 30 seconds each, doing as many moves as possible.

Coaching Points

This is an excellent coaching tactic for work on all bottom maneuvers: stand-ups, switches, sit-out series, Granby rolls, hip heists, and so on. At the conclusion of practice, stress shadow wrestling off the bottom to work on quickness and endurance. Again, always watch for common errors as they shadow wrestle in the bottom or defensive position.

GAME 1: THE KNEE SLAP

Setup

The partners start in the neutral position.

Action

Each wrestler reaches in and tries to slap his partner's knees, focusing on slapping the lead knee. Each wrestler is awarded a point when he slaps his partner's knee hard.

Coaching Point

Stress that the wrestlers be light on their feet, quickly moving backward when their partners attempt to slap.

GAME 2: THE FOOT TAG

Setup

In the neutral position, each wrestler locks his hands behind his back.

Action

On the whistle, the partners try to step on each other's feet, keeping track of who scores the most points.

Coaching Point

Stress the importance of quickness when performing this drill.

GAME 3: MULTIPLE QUICKNESS AND AGILITY ACTIVITIES

Setup

The coach can invent all kinds of agility and quickness drills by putting the wrestlers in different situations.

Action

In practice, make up a wrestling situation for the athletes to act out then blow the whistle. Following are three ideas for such agility and quickness situation drills.

The Quick Stand

Have the wrestlers lie on their backs, side by side, in opposite directions (*a*). On the whistle, the wrestlers quickly come to the standing position. The partner who gets to his feet first scores a point.

The Leg Break Away

Have each wrestler hold one of his partner's legs, facing the partner (*b*). On the whistle, the wrestlers attempt to break away from each other. The partner who breaks away first scores the point.

The Double-Cradle Fight

Have the partners cradle each other (*c*). On the whistle, the wrestler who wins the cradle battle scores.

Coaching Point

Allow the wrestlers to compete full speed for a few seconds. During this time, emphasize the importance of quickness, agility, balance, and proper technique when wrestling maneuvers are performed.

REACTION

Setup

Wrestlers stand in lines facing the coach.

Action

When the coach points to the left, the wrestlers throw the right leg back. Next, when the coach motions to the right, the wrestlers throw the left leg back. When the coach points to himself, the wrestlers change levels and penetrate toward the coach. And finally, when the coach points to the wrestlers, they scoot backward.

Coaching Point

Stress quickness and proper technique when performing the penetration part of the drill.

SPIN FOR CONDITIONING

Setup

With one partner on all fours, the top partner puts his chest on the bottom man's back.

Action

On the whistle, the top man spins in one direction, changing direction when the coach blows the whistle. This drill should last approximately 30 seconds for each partner.

Common Error

Encourage the top man to stay off his knees while moving left or right. It's a common error when the wrestlers begin to become fatigued.

HIP-HEIST

Setup

In this solitary drill, the wrestler starts on his toes and hands with belly up (*a*).

Action

The wrestler does a series of hip heists on the mat, hip-heisting one direction and then the other (*b* and *c*). Alternatively, the wrestler does a series of moves that involve starting from the feet. He takes a penetration step, then sprawls, and finally performs a hip heist.

Common Error

When performing this drill, the wrestler's legs must hip-heist under each other, never over each other—a common error when performing this activity.

WRESTLING ENDURANCE DRILLS

Becoming a champion is like wrestling a gorilla. You don't stop when you get tired—you stop when the gorilla gets tired.

Robert Strauss

I think that endurance for wrestling comes primarily from wrestling. An athlete can build up a lot of endurance by hard drilling of wrestling moves and a lot of live wrestling. If a wrestler stays active during most of his daily practices, he will naturally get into shape.

I believe in alternating hard workouts with moderate, less strenuous workouts so that the wrestlers have a chance to recover and rebuild. Endurance drills can be varied by their level of difficulty and length, depending on how hard you want to push your wrestlers.

The following are endurance (or toughness) drills that you can choose for your practice sessions.

Shadow Wrestling   The wrestlers should perform the drill described earlier in the chapter at the end of practice for endurance. It should last 30 seconds or more and be repeated up to three times in the neutral position and then on the bottom position.

Chain Wrestling   Although this is an outstanding activity for promoting technique, it can also be used as a drill to increase endurance. I like this drill because it helps wrestlers avoid mental breakdowns (losing concentration, forgetting to continue movement by acting and reacting, and so on).

This drill should last anywhere from 30 seconds to two minutes. Chain wrestling is discussed in greater depth in chapter 9.

Black Flag Day   This activity allows wrestlers to devote an entire practice to "doing their own thing." The wrestlers are required to work out continuously for approximately an hour, performing any physical wrestling-oriented activity of their choosing. Not only is this a great way to promote overall conditioning, but it allows the wrestlers the freedom to do what they want the entire practice, as long as they keep moving. They can do skill drilling as long as they wish or wrestle competitively until the end of practice. This activity is great for varying practice late in the season. The change of pace helps in eliminating staleness. It is a hard practice, but the tough wrestlers really like it.

IRONMAN

Setup

The participants start in a neutral tie-up position.

Action

The drill includes full-contact tie-ups, pushing and shoving your partner for 20 to 30 seconds. A variation involves the wrestlers trying to drive each other out of the circle. The wrestler who forces his opponent out of the circle or snaps him down to his hand(s) or knee(s) receives a point.

Coaching Point

This drill encourages mental and physical toughness and aggressiveness. Emphasize that the wrestlers should be very physical, almost to the point of fighting.

Common Error

Of course, you must monitor this drill carefully. The coach should make certain that the wrestlers keep their physical and mental composure.

PUMMELING

Setup

The wrestlers start in the overhook and underhook neutral position, chest to chest.

Action

On the whistle, each partner works for underhooks while pushing into the other partner. This aggressive activity should last 30 seconds or more and be repeated by each partner up to three times.

Coaching Points

Do not allow the wrestlers to attempt throws or takedowns; just pummeling should occur. This drill is a great way to keep the sweat going. Use this drill as a warm-up activity, starting slowly and gradually becoming more intense. It is a good way to warm up the chest, arms, and shoulders. The activity is also appropriate at the end of practice.

HEAVY ROPE TRAINING

Heavy rope training has gathered much interest in the exercise world in recent years. The number of drills that can be done with a heavy rope are almost limitless, and the only constraint is one's creativity.

The basic stance for heavy ropes is a square wrestling stance (quarter squat position). The stance can be modified into lunging, kneeling, or sitting. However, we are going to focus on the wrestling stance.

The following is a sampling of five heavy rope drills that will work nicely in a wrestler's development. The drills should be done for a minimum of 30 seconds, with the same amount (or less) of rest between each drill. Be sure the wrestlers warm up (going slowly) before you go into the 30-second interval.

1. Alternating Ripple Effect

In the wrestling square stance, the wrestler alternates each arm up and down to create waves.

2. In-Unison Ripple Effect

In the wrestling square stance, the wrestler moves both arms up and down together to create waves.

3. Slam

In the wrestling square stance, the wrestler alternates each arm up and down to create waves. On the coach's signal, the wrestler slams the ropes to the floor.

4. Lunge

The wrestler lunges forward every few seconds while maintaining ripples.

5. Stepping

The wrestler steps up and down on a bench in front of him while maintaining ripples.

As previously mentioned, you can develop your own heavy rope drills to fit the needs of your wrestlers.

CONCLUSION

After a lively practice workout filled with vigorous conditioning drills, a cool-down period is mandatory. We finish our more strenuous practices by having the wrestlers walk around the mat room several times to cool down.

I also believe that "draining the legs" is important. We have each wrestler lie on his back with his buttocks against the wall and his feet as high as possible against the wall. It is my belief that this resting position promotes blood flow back to the heart and fresh legs for the next day.

It is also a great idea for wrestlers to do some additional stretching, receive additional wrestling instruction, or get a pep talk from the coaches. Humor is also a great way to conclude practice, along with an orange or popsicle treat.

Chapter 9 offers the coach sound practice formats in which drills are an integral facet of the workout session. It also presents a practice evaluation strategy and many other practice components. Finally, chapter 9 outlines an off-season agenda for developing the successful wrestling program that every coach must promote.

Effective Practices and Off-Season Activities

Bill Welker

" *Progress always involves risk; you can't steal second base and keep your foot on first.* "

Frederick Wilcox

The success of your scholastic wrestling program will depend largely on how well you prepare practice sessions from day to day. Daily practices must evolve with the needs of the athletes participating in the program. For example, if you are working with young and inexperienced wrestlers, you will need to spend more time on the perfection of fundamental techniques. After that, you can begin to move on to more advanced wrestling skills.

PRESEASON DAILY PRACTICE SESSIONS

Many state high school associations designate dates when participating schools may begin organized wrestling practices. Because a six-week training period is considered ideal in preparing wrestlers for competitive action, it would be to your advantage to schedule dual meets and tournaments to allow for at least this amount of preseason practice time.

Preseason practices should start with conditioning activities and passive to semiactive drill work. In the first two weeks of practice, emphasis should be on preparing the wrestlers for wrestling.

Following are some examples of conditioning drills for strength, quickness, agility, endurance, flexibility, balance, and mental toughness that can be implemented during preseason practices:

- Strength: Big 10, weight-room lifting, and rope climbing (chapter 8).
- Quickness, agility, flexibility, and balance (see chapter 2): Spin drill (see chapter 1), stretching exercises, shadow wrestling (on feet and bottom), quickness and agility games, hip heist, and rope skipping (see chapter 8).
- Endurance and mental toughness: stair running, Ironman drill, and LOBO round-up (see chapter 8).

Always remember, if you begin active wrestling before the participants are properly conditioned, you may find yourself facing an abundance of injuries. Moreover, when you do begin all-out wrestling in practice, it would be wise to start with mat (or ground) wrestling and gradually work into active takedown wrestling.

This is also the time of year you will want to work on your wrestlers' fundamental skills, discuss rule changes, and review healthy weight-management practices. Keeping with this philosophy from the beginning of the year will make for a safer and more rewarding season.

IN-SEASON DAILY PRACTICE SESSIONS

The last two weeks of preseason practice should resemble your in-season practice sessions. At this point in the year, you shouldn't teach any new moves; instead, stress the perfection of previously taught maneuvers via drills and active wrestling.

The wrestling workout session is the most important phase of practice for two reasons. First, it allows you the opportunity to observe the wrestlers more thoroughly and correct their weak areas. Second, it is the best conditioning activity for preparing your wrestlers for competitive action.

On days before dual meets or tournaments, practice should be very light so the wrestlers get sufficient rest for their matches. A few conditioning exercises and wrestling drills would be adequate. If the dual meet or tournament begins early the next day, a discussion period and pep talk would suffice.

Of course, those wrestlers with weight-management problems may have to do additional work. This would include endurance activities, such as rope skipping, interval running, or riding the stationary bike to make weight. However, they should be close to match weight the day before competition. They should spend this time thinking about their opponents and wrestling, not thinking about food and making weight. If a wrestler is constantly dwelling on weight problems, you must step in and sternly suggest that he move up a weight class for his own physical and psychological well-being.

At the start of practices that follow a dual meet or tournament, point out mistakes made by individual wrestlers. They may need to work on their bridging skills, in which case you would reteach the half nelson bridging counter with partner drill (see chapter 6). Or if they had trouble countering the double-leg takedown, you might revisit the double-leg reaction counter drill (see chapter 3).

On the flip side, don't forget to praise those team members who had superior performances.

PRESEASON AND IN-SEASON PRACTICE FORMAT

The following format demonstrates the similarities and differences between preseason and in-season practices. Keep in mind, preseason practice emphasis should be on conditioning and review of wrestling moves and development of new moves; in-season practice consists of longer wrestling workout sessions as well as move instruction based on scouting reports regarding upcoming opponents. In both cases, daily practices should never last more than two hours. After that point, scholastic wrestlers tend to lose their ability to concentrate.

- **Conditioning warm-up exercises (10 to 15 minutes).** These exercises should stress total-body flexibility, strength, and endurance. Such training will help prevent injuries. The same warm-up should be used for both preseason and in-season practices.
- **Wrestling drill work (10 to 15 minutes).** Passive to active drills involving skills and moves from all facets of wrestling are the priority during this phase of practice. Use this approach in both preseason and in-season practice.
- **Step-by-step analysis of wrestling moves (10 to 15 minutes).** In this phase, thoroughly demonstrate moves; then let the wrestlers practice the maneuvers' essential parts step by step. Use this technique often in preseason practices but only when necessary during in-season practices.
- **Wrestling workout sessions (30 to 60 minutes).** The wrestling workout sessions should be much more intense during in-season practices when wrestler conditioning is at its peak. Preseason workouts should last about 30 minutes; in-season wrestling workout sessions should last for nearly an hour. During this time, divide the wrestlers into groups. While one group is wrestling, the other group is running and weight training. Thus, no one is standing around while others are wrestling. (If your wrestlers do lift weights, it should be every other day.)

  During the wrestling workout sessions, you should frequently stop wrestlers in the middle of action with two purposes in mind. First, show the wrestlers how they are inadequately executing moves. Second, if necessary, demonstrate another move that would be more suitable for the same situation. Keep in mind, the wrestling workout sessions are the most important phase of in-season practices.
- **Conditioning finish exercises (10 to 15 minutes).** These end-of-practice exercises should be snappy, with emphasis on strength and endurance skills. This phase would be identical for both preseason and in-season practices.

Never forget that as a coach, you are also a teacher. You should always entertain any questions from your wrestlers regarding practice drills and moves. If a wrestler does not understand the significance of what he is doing, successful accomplishment of a maneuver will rarely be the result. The following are several teaching tips to ensure your practices are meaningful and produce winning results.

Teaching New Moves

When teaching a new move to your wrestlers, you should be able to do the maneuver flawlessly yourself. A step-by-step analysis of the move is your best approach. Emphasize those aspects of the maneuver that make it effective in competition.

Also, stress *why* a move should be drilled in a certain manner, and what could happen if it is not. The more profound understanding your wrestlers have regarding the purpose behind each move, the easier it will be for them to master it.

The adept wrestling coach never attempts to demonstrate a move he does not fully understand. There is no shame in admitting to your wrestlers that you will need to do some research involving a certain wrestling skill. Your athletes will respect this course of action much more than if you feign knowledge of a move. In fact, you could easily harm your wrestlers' performance by showing a move you don't know authoritatively.

Avoiding Staleness

Staleness in practice may be defined as that time in the season when the wrestlers appear sluggish and seem to be regressing in their wrestling skills. This phenomenon usually occurs midway through the season. You can take two courses of action to alleviate the problem: First, give your wrestlers a day off from practice. This will revitalize their attitudes and focus their thoughts. Second, devote one practice to an activity the wrestlers will enjoy that is completely unrelated to wrestling. For example, they might play a game of crab soccer or have an arm-wrestling tournament during practice, and then be sent home for the day. (Refer to chapter 8 for additional conditioning activities for allaying staleness.)

Promoting Cooperation and Competition in Practice

Cooperation and competition are both intricate aspects of a successful and productive wrestling program. Cooperation may take the form of the more experienced wrestlers helping novice wrestlers correctly drill the many wrestling skills they need to learn. Also, various drills entail a cooperative effort in which one wrestler offers the proper resistance for correct performance of a drill.

Of course, the most important element for producing championship programs is practice competition. The more a wrestler is pushed in practice, the better he will perform in dual meets and tournaments. Without question, promoting a competitive spirit in your daily workout sessions can never be overemphasized.

It is very difficult to distinguish between cooperation and competition in the practice setting. When you have developed a competitive attitude in your team, each member will complement the others by exhibiting maximum effort at practice. In other words, two practice partners, competitively motivated, are cooperating with each other by pushing each other and striving to be the best.

Just as cooperation and competition are important factors in the classroom, the same should be true in the practice room. You can and should incorporate many classroom strategies and techniques into your daily practice sessions. Your wrestling program must include the following:

- Well-structured practice plans
- Competent demonstrations of drilling moves by the coach
- Knowledge of how to combat practice staleness
- An understanding of the relationship between cooperation and competition in the realm of daily practices

SPECIALIZED WRESTLING WORKOUTS

The typical wrestling workout session involves spending about 50 percent of the time in the neutral position perfecting takedown skills. This is a smart workout approach because of the great importance takedown superiority has for winning matches. Next, both bottom and top mat wrestling would be equally divided for the purpose of polishing escape or reversal and ride or pinning combination skills.

Likewise, for a change of pace you will sometimes want to incorporate workouts that add variation to the traditional wrestling session. Chain wrestling, situation wrestling, round-robin wrestling, and blindfold wrestling are excellent alternatives described in the following pages.

Chain Wrestling

Too often in contemporary scholastic matches, the bottom wrestler will attempt to escape or reverse his opponent by using only one or two moves. If they don't work, his opponent ultimately ends up riding him. We seem to have forgotten a lost art—chain wrestling, a fast-paced bottom maneuver and top countermaneuver wrestling activity. After perfecting the moves and countermoves that follow, you can incorporate chain wrestling. The most common chain wrestling skills include the following multiple moves:

Standard Chain Wrestling Workout

Step 1	Sit-out to turn-in (bottom wrestler)
	Follow sit-out to turn-in (top wrestler)
Step 2	Sit-out to turn-out (bottom wrestler)
	Follow sit-out to turn-out (top wrestler)
Step 3	Switch (bottom wrestler)
	Reswitch (top wrestler)
Step 4	Side roll (bottom wrestler)
	Re-side roll (top wrestler)

Step 5   Granby roll (bottom wrestler)

Granby roll follow-through on head (top wrestler)

Step 6   Stand-up (bottom wrestler)

Back heel trip to mat (top wrestler)

Wrestlers repeat this chain wrestling process as many times as you instruct (usually three to five cycles) with wrestler W1 on the bottom. Then wrestler W2 would assume the bottom position, repeating the cycle the same number of times.

Of course, you may develop variations to this chain wrestling format to suit your particular mat wrestling concerns. No matter how you plan your chain wrestling activity, the key purpose of the workout is to train the bottom wrestler not to stop after one or two moves.

Another benefit of chain wrestling is that it teaches the top wrestler how to follow moves performed by the bottom wrestler. Likewise, it is a superb conditioning tool for workout sessions. You may even want to create a practice competition out of chain wrestling, timing the wrestlers to see which pair is fastest in completing the cycles.

In recent decades, coaches have placed so much emphasis on takedowns that many have ignored the importance of moving on the bottom. Chain wrestling is a snappy workout activity that doesn't take much practice time and leads to improved mat wrestling.

Situation Wrestling

Situation wrestling is usually incorporated during the season. It is much like a regular workout session with one exception: The wrestlers are placed in various wrestling positions and begin wrestling from that point. As with typical wrestling workouts, periodically stop the wrestlers to demonstrate what they are doing wrong.

There is a twofold purpose for including situation wrestling in daily practice sessions. First, you can use the strategy to work on new moves and to demonstrate how they should be performed during real wrestling situations.

The second rationale for adding situation wrestling to practice plans involves the scouting phase of coaching. While scouting rival teams, the coach often observes certain moves that members of those squads use the most to score points. Wisely, the coach will place his wrestlers in those various move situations, having them counter the maneuvers in preparation for an upcoming dual meet or tournament. This wrestling strategy has been very successful over the years.

Let's now consider two examples of situation wrestling—one to perfect new moves and the other to prepare for competition.

Drilling a New Move

The coach has just completed demonstrating the standing suicide switch reversal maneuver. At this point, the wrestlers perform the maneuver in the following manner:

1. After standing up, the bottom wrestler fakes a standing switch, turning from one side to the other.
2. Then the bottom wrestler drops forward to the mat head first.
3. Finally, just before the bottom wrestler's head hits the mat, he executes a quick hip-heist switch, scoring the reversal.

After the wrestlers passively perform the move, the coach then places the wrestlers in the standing position and blows the whistle. With the top wrestler resisting fully, the bottom wrestler is given 15 seconds to complete the standing suicide switch. This is an all-out burst of wrestling effort by both wrestlers, with the coach periodically stopping the action to correct mistakes.

Drilling for Competition

When scouting the next opponent in a dual meet, the coach learns that the majority of wrestlers are very proficient at scoring double-leg takedowns.

At practices leading up to the meet, the coach places the wrestlers in the neutral position. He instructs the attacking team members to deeply penetrate the opponents' defense, clamping their hands around the knees.

On the whistle, the wrestlers defend themselves from the double-leg takedown counter, performing the following steps:

Step 1   Crossface and sprawl
Step 2   Whizzer and hip into opponent with whipping action
Step 3   Force head down with free hand and push away

This process continues until all practice partners have demonstrated the ability to properly counter the double-leg takedown.

Situation wrestling will greatly enhance the skill level of all team members. Do not fail to make it part of your workout repertoire.

Round-Robin Wrestling

Round-robin wrestling is another action-packed workout. One advantage to round-robin wrestling is that the entire squad participates simultaneously. This routine involves the following procedure:

1. Divide the team into groups of five wrestlers each whose weight is as similar to each other as possible.
2. Assign a number from 1 to 5 to each wrestler in the group.

3. Wrestler 1 steps in the center of his group. He is given 30 seconds to score a takedown on each member of his group in the following order:
   - Wrestler 1 vs. wrestler 2
   - Wrestler 1 vs. wrestler 3
   - Wrestler 1 vs. wrestler 4
   - Wrestler 1 vs. wrestler 5

4. If a takedown is scored in less than 30 seconds, the participants stand up and go at it again (and again) until time has expired.

5. Then wrestler 2 does the same with wrestlers 3, 4, 5, and 1. The process continues until everyone in the group has spent his time in the middle.

6. This round-robin session would include wrestling in the referee's position, emphasizing escapes, reversals, rides, or pinning combinations.

7. The inactive wrestlers for each group may act as spotters, protecting the active wrestlers from going out of bounds or colliding with other pairs.

As you can visualize, round-robin wrestling consists of a very invigorating workout. The prime objectives are quite obvious: conditioning and further skill development. Following are some interesting variations that make this alternative wrestling strategy even more intriguing:

1. Each group member as the primary wrestler would be required to counter maneuvers directed toward him by his round-robin rival, per covert instructions given to his practice opponents from the coach. This would encompass countermoves from both the neutral and referee's (bottom and top) positions.

2. The inactive wrestlers in the group could be instructed to run in place, rather than just observe.

3. The coach could include an intragroup competition of the round-robin exercise, for example, by keeping track of who has the most takedowns in each group during the session workout. One appropriate incentive would be to exempt the winning wrestlers from closing exercises.

Of course, the creative coach may come up with even more novel approaches to enhance the round-robin experience. That's fantastic! Just remember to follow the previous guidelines, and it will be a productive substitute to the traditional workout scheme.

Blindfold Wrestling

Blindfold wrestling is another beneficial innovation for practices. The workout session is the same as usual, with one exception: The wrestlers are blindfolded. Though the wrestlers may be a little hesitant at first, they will soon realize that they really don't need their eyes in order to wrestle.

Proper body positioning in wrestling is really a matter of feel, a sense of where you are or should be. Of course, such mat sense can be achieved only via years of practice. Note that it is important for the veteran wrestlers on the team to assist the younger wrestlers performing this specialized workout. Blindfold wrestling is one workout medium a coach can implement to achieve this wrestler-oriented goal. The only props needed are blindfolds cut from old bed sheets or bandannas. The following are a few basic guidelines for incorporating blindfold wrestling into your daily practices:

1. When introducing the wrestlers to blindfold wrestling, blindfold only one of the wrestlers in each pair. The sighted wrestler will help keep his opponent from going out of bounds.

2. After both wrestlers have experienced being alternately blindfolded and feel comfortable with the technique, blindfold both of them.

3. To start in the neutral position, the two wrestlers will use the fingertouch method as described in rule 6 of the *NFHS Wrestling Rules Book*. This will also prepare the wrestlers should they ever have to compete against a wrestler with impaired vision.

4. No variations are needed for the referee's position, even if the optional offensive starting position is used.

5. The wrestlers must stay in continuous contact with each other throughout the entire workout.

Be sure to take safety measures into consideration. First, during blindfold wrestling, there should be fewer wrestling pairs competing on the mats than usual. Second, those wrestlers waiting to work out must act as spotters, stopping their peers as they are about to go out of bounds. Third, these wrestlers should also lead the blindfolded wrestlers back to their starting positions and restart them. Finally, the coach's whistle must be the signal for all blindfolded wrestlers to stop immediately.

During a blindfold wrestling session, the coach should stop the wrestlers and ask them what they are experiencing. The most common response will be that the wrestlers found themselves reacting to their opponents' movements rather than thinking about what to do.

You will learn by watching whether your wrestlers are responding properly and swiftly, relying primarily on their sense of touch rather than sight. As we all know, this tactile (or mat) sense is a characteristic observed in all champion wrestlers.

Chain wrestling, situation wrestling, round-robin wrestling, and blindfold wrestling have a great deal to add to a comprehensive wrestling program. These workout alternatives increase stamina, develop continuous mat (or ground) wrestling abilities, improve takedown skills, promote mat sense, and further prepare the wrestlers for competition.

Practice Wrestle-Offs

Your wrestle-off matches determine who will compete on the varsity squad. To begin with, it would be very wise to use registered officials for a wrestle-off, which should be conducted as though it is a real competitive match. This practice will dismiss any thoughts by the participants or their parents that you show favoritism, especially with closely contested wrestle-offs.

Your initial wrestle-off matches should occur at least two weeks before your first scheduled meet. They should be conducted with the same formality found in dual meets and tournament bouts. In fact, you could conduct the wrestle-off matches during "Meet the Team" night.

If two wrestlers are evenly matched, the best-out-of-three-matches format would be advisable. This setup leaves fewer questions in the minds of the competing wrestlers or you as to who is the more competent wrestler.

All wrestle-off matches should be carefully evaluated. With this feedback, both wrestlers can learn about their strong and weak points. After the first set of wrestle-offs, encourage wrestlers to challenge their varsity counterparts throughout the remainder of the season. A wrestling program that promotes wrestle-off matches adds to the competitive spirit of the participants and keeps everyone on their toes.

One final point needs to be mentioned. There may be isolated instances when you must decide who wrestles varsity, even if your choice is not the winner of wrestle-offs. How can this be? Well, there are those athletes who are great competitors in the practice room. However, they have stage fright in front of the fans. In essence, they are great wrestling-room competitors but freeze during actual dual meets and tournament events. It is a tough call to make, but sometimes it has to be done for the good of the team.

GROUP WORK DURING PRACTICE

Group work aids in a smooth, well-organized, and fast-paced wrestling practice. Group work is usually a necessity because the practice room cannot accommodate the entire squad at one time. This is especially true during wrestling workout sessions and sometimes with the specialized conditioning drills found in chapter 8.

Since most successful wrestling programs consist of 30 to 40 team members, there is no need for more than two groups during the wrestling workout phase. The ideal number of group members would be 18 to 20 wrestlers. Of course, team size ultimately determines the number of groups.

When dividing your squad into groups, see to it that the primary group is composed mainly of your varsity performers. The other groups would be made up of the less polished wrestlers. You definitely want the members of each group evenly matched by weight and ability.

When one group is wrestling, the other groups could be running in the gym or outside or lifting weights. However, if the gym is occupied, and the weather does not permit them to run outside, an alternative could be jumping rope or running in place, with jog and sprint intervals.

Assign two or three student leaders in each group to keep the participants "stepping" and motivated when they are not involved in wrestling or otherwise in front of the vigilant eyes of the coaches. These student leaders should be very conscientious individuals who are highly respected by their peers on the team.

Group work reduces boredom in practice. Furthermore, group work assists in eliminating down time in practice. It also allows the coaches an opportunity for more individualized instruction.

Varsity Wrestlers

First and foremost, your varsity competitors are the "prime beef" of the wrestling squad. Since your most important goal as a successful coach is to develop winning teams, more individual attention must be given to your varsity wrestlers.

The varsity performers should always receive additional attention during practice, especially during the wrestling workout sessions. In fact, their workout sessions must be more comprehensive and intense than the rest of the wrestling squad. This does not mean you are intentionally neglecting the junior varsity participants. However, because of the limited amount of daily practice time, your focus must be on the varsity wrestlers.

Junior Varsity Wrestlers

Although less practice time is devoted to the junior varsity or reserve wrestlers, this does not mean that you, as coaches, ignore these participants. In truth, they are the wrestling team's future.

When I began as an assistant coach, I was put in charge of teaching the junior varsity wrestlers. My job was to keep them busy, and more important, motivated in their efforts to improve wrestling skills.

The first matter I undertook was to find a vacant room or area in the school to work exclusively with these lesser-skilled participants. I accomplished this task. In doing so, I was able to provide the valuable mat time that these wrestlers so desperately needed.

Second, the majority of my coaching time was devoted to teaching the basic, essential wrestling skills. This individualized instruction kept them actively involved in skill improvement. They also realized that the coaching staff sincerely cared about them and their efforts.

Finally, I fashioned a very aggressive schedule for the junior varsity team members. There was always a complete junior varsity dual meet scheduled prior to the varsity meet. If an opposing team had few reserve wrestlers, I invited novice wrestlers from other schools to fill in the open weight classes. Rival coaches were elated with the offer to give their wrestlers more wrestling experience.

We also hosted and competed in several junior varsity tournaments throughout the season. Our goals for these wrestlers were achieved. They were kept busy and very enthusiastic about their competitive schedule. The result was that many of them went on to become future state champions and state place winners.

Many factors lead to the creation of a successful wrestling program. An understanding of the significance regarding the areas previously discussed provides for a rewarding coaching experience. It is also an enjoyable and positive adventure for the most significant members of any wrestling program: the wrestlers.

OVERLAPPING SPORT SEASONS

In most schools throughout the United States, football and soccer, as well as other fall sports, end anywhere from one to three weeks after wrestling practices have begun. Should a fall team make the state playoffs, the wrestlers may be absent from practice even longer.

Thus, a number of your multisport wrestlers have missed hours of vital wrestling instruction time. To combat this dilemma, have your assistant coaches take these late arrivals aside and review skills already emphasized in practice. Of course, you must understand that this quick-study approach will not be as detailed due to the limited time. Still, at the very least, the wrestlers who were involved in fall sports will be brought up to date with the rest of the team.

There is another matter that must be taken into account. Although the athletes involved in the fall sports are in fairly good shape, it is definitely not the same as wrestling. (Nothing is.) They will need, at the very least, a week of intense conditioning skills and drill work before they can commence with all-out wrestling. Most state high school associations have a required number of practices that wrestlers who start late must have attended before they may compete.

As is often the case, some of your best wrestlers participate in fall sports. It would be disappointing to lose a good wrestler to injury because he was not given the proper amount of practice time to fully condition himself for full-speed wrestling.

EVALUATING PRACTICES

To have a successful program, you must develop practice sessions that benefit each wrestler. You need to match practice strategies with the wrestlers' ability levels. Here are general questions you want to ask yourself after each practice:

- Did the wrestlers react well performing today's drills?
- Were the wrestlers able to adapt to new moves taught?
- Were the wrestlers giving all they had during practice workout sessions?
- Were partners in the groups cooperating during the drill and new move phase of practice?
- Was each group working to its fullest during the off-mat activities phase of practice?
- Do we need to spend more time with drill work, workout sessions, conditioning, and so on?
- Did the wrestlers seem stale during practice?
- Do the wrestlers need a day off or a change of pace in their activities?
- Was the overall practice successful in achieving the daily objectives and goals?

On a more detailed basis, you must continually watch for wrestler strengths, but more important, wrestlers' weaknesses. Always be aware of wrestlers' mistakes and correct them immediately. The following is a sample checklist of weaknesses to eliminate in the three wrestling positions.

Neutral Position

The wrestler is crossing his feet (foot work). _____

The wrestler's feet are much too close together or too far apart. _____

The wrestler is standing up too straight (lower center of gravity, the hips). _____

The wrestler has his elbows out too far. _____

The wrestler is reaching for his opponent rather than penetrating. _____

The wrestler is looking at his opponent's face or feet instead of focusing attention on his opponent's center of gravity (hips). _____

The wrestler is backing away from his opponent. _____

The wrestler is not crossfacing properly. _____

The wrestler is not sprawling on his toes. _____

The wrestler is putting too much weight on his heels. _____

Offensive (Top) Position

The wrestler is reaching over his opponent's shoulder.   _____

The wrestler is riding too high (readjust center of gravity, the hips).   _____

The wrestler is not on his toes while riding opponent.   _____

The wrestler is locking hands on the mat.   _____

The wrestler is pulling his opponent on top of him instead of riding with weight pressured on his opponent.   _____

The wrestler is too parallel while riding or pinning his opponent.   _____

The wrestler has his head too far over his opponent's back on the far side.   _____

The wrestler has all his weight on his knees while riding his opponent.   _____

The wrestler is repeatedly assuming an incorrect starting position on top.   _____

The wrestler reacts too slowly on top when the whistle blows.   _____

Defensive (Bottom) Position

The wrestler is reaching over his opponent's back while executing a switch.   _____

The wrestler is stopping after one move.   _____

The wrestler is sitting-out too far.   _____

The wrestler is not changing direction.   _____

The wrestler is balling up, making him easy prey for a cradle.   _____

The wrestler is not controlling his opponent's hands when standing up.   _____

The wrestler is leaning too far forward when assuming the referee's position (lower center of gravity, the hips).   _____

The wrestler is lying on his belly with elbows close to his body.   _____

The wrestler is looking toward his opponent's half nelson.   _____

The wrestler is hesitating on the bottom when the whistle blows (needs to curl toes).   _____

Remember, you must correct wrestlers' mistakes as soon as possible. If not, those mistakes will become bad habits. However, there is one exception regarding the evaluation of wrestlers during practice: individual wrestler creativity.

To be a perceptive coach, you must have the wisdom to accept the uniqueness of all wrestlers on your team. In fact, you will sometimes need to compromise when interacting with your athletes. Consider the following.

When your wrestlers begin to perfect their essential wrestling skills, you may observe a wrestler who is unconsciously adding a subtle variation to a specific move he has learned. Furthermore, he is having a high degree of success with the maneuver. Should you stop it? No. As long as the variation is, for the most part, fundamentally sound, let it be.

Occasionally, a slight modification of a move may be very appropriate for the body type of a specific wrestler. However, if a move's variation involves a bad habit that could potentially get the wrestler in trouble, do not hesitate to break him of it.

Individual wrestler creativity can also be a valuable learning experience for the coach. A good analogy would be the high school math instructor who shows his class how to solve some problems assigned for homework. As he is checking papers the next day, the teacher finds that one student devised his own alternative method for solving the problems, one that is also fundamentally sound. Thus, both the teacher and student learn. Such is often the case when coaching wrestlers with unique physical abilities.

MODELS FOR DAILY PRACTICES

The following are examples of three daily practice plans developed for the wrestlers. They illustrate practice plans for preseason, in-season, and activities.

Preseason Practice Model

Keep in mind, preseason practices should stress getting the wrestlers in competitive condition. Emphasis should be placed on drill work and the instruction of moves (old and new). The following is a typical preseason practice model:

I. Starting Practice: Flexibility and Conditioning Exercises (10 to 15 minutes)

A. Neck circles and four-way neck exercises _____

B. Arm circles _____

C. Wrist and ankle circles _____

D. Belly circles _____

E. Leg stretches _____

F. Ankle circles _____

G. Bridging (side to side and backward and forward) _____

H. Push-ups _____

I. Run and front roll intervals _____

II. Wrestling Drill Work (15 minutes)

A. Penetration drill   _____

B. Push-pull drill   _____

C. Spin drill to snap-down drill   _____

D. Hip-heist drill   _____

III. Teach New Move or Review Move (15 minutes)

A. Use step-by-step analysis of moves so wrestlers understand why and how they work.

    1. Fireman's carry instruction   _____

    2. Standing Peterson roll instruction   _____

    3. Crossface-cradle instruction   _____

IV. Wrestling Workout Session (30 minutes)

A. Neutral position (60% of wrestling workout session)   _____

B. Starting in referee's position: offensive and defensive position (40% of wrestling workout session)   _____

C. If group work is needed due to mat space, each group would work out for 15 minutes. While one group is working out, the other group could be running, lifting weights, climbing ropes, and so on.   _____

V. Finishing Practice: Conditioning Exercises (10 to 15 minutes)

A. Run for 10 minutes (sprint and jog intervals) or jump rope   _____

B. Strength exercises (such as sit-ups, push-ups, pull-ups on bar)   _____

C. Chalk talk as wrestlers cool down   _____

IN-SEASON PRACTICE MODEL

The most important phase of in-season practices is the workout session. The drill work session should place emphasis on neutral, offensive, and defensive areas based on scouting reports. During this point in the season, the new or review move instruction phase is virtually nonexistent unless there is an important maneuver that needs to be reviewed. The following is a model in-season lesson plan that will keep your wrestlers constantly ready for competitive action.

I. Starting Practice: Flexibility and Conditioning Exercises
(10 to 15 minutes)

A. Neck circles and four-way neck exercises   _____

B. Arm circles   _____

C. Wrist and ankle circles   _____

D. Belly circles   _____

E. Leg stretches   _____

F. Ankle circles   _____

G. Bridging (side to side and backward and forward)   _____

H. Push-ups   _____

 I. Run and front roll intervals   _____

II. Wrestling Drill Work (10 minutes)

A. Sprawl drill   _____

B. Ankle-waist drill on whistle   _____

C. Spin drill to snap-down drill   _____

D. Stand-up (hand control) drill   _____

IV. Wrestling Workout Session (60 minutes)

A. Neutral position (50% of time)   _____

B. Starting in referee's position: offensive and defensive position
(50% of time)   _____

C. If group work is needed because of limited mat space,
each group would work out for 30 minutes. While one group
is working out, the other group could be running, lifting
weights, climbing ropes, and so on. (Note: At this point
in the season, you can incorporate specialized workouts:
chain wrestling, situation wrestling, round-robin wrestling,
and blindfold wrestling as illustrated in this chapter.)   _____

V. Finishing Practice: Conditioning Exercises
(10 to 15 minutes)

A. Run for 10 minutes (sprint and jog intervals) or jump rope   _____

B. Strength exercises (such as sit-ups, push-ups, pull-ups on bar)   _____

C. Chalk talk as wrestlers cool down   _____

ACTIVITIES PRACTICE MODEL

As previously mentioned, sometimes during midseason the wrestlers may seem to be in a rut. This staleness may be due to the boredom of repetition from practice to practice. Thus, you would be wise to devise an activities day where the wrestlers can have competitive fun. The following is a model of an activities day practice:

I. Starting Practice: Flexibility Exercises (5 minutes)

A. Neck circles and four-way neck exercises   _____

B. Arm circles   _____

C. Wrist and ankle circles   _____

D. Belly circles   _____

E. Leg stretches   _____

F. Ankle circles   _____

II. Activities Competition (30 minutes)

Directions: Divide the wrestlers into partners who are evenly matched by weight class and wrestling ability. The wrestler who scores the most points performing the activities wins.

A. The knee slap   _____

B. Foot tag   _____

C. The quick stand   _____

D. The double-cradle fight   _____

(Note: All of the preceding game activities can be found in chapter 8.)

III. Early Dismissal

The coach sends the wrestlers home after enjoying a short change-of-pace practice.   _____

The preceding models will assist you in developing your own practice plans. Of course, you may need to make variations to your practice plans to fit the specific needs and ability levels of your wrestlers. The important point is that you create practice plans that will be of the most benefit to your squad.

OFF-SEASON ACTIVITIES

The dedicated wrestler does not stop learning and training when the last practice of the season ends. He is continually looking for ways to improve his wrestling skills, muscle tone, and cardiorespiratory endurance. These objectives can be accomplished through a variety of activities during the postseason months. The following are off-season priorities for the aspiring state champion: summer wrestling clinics, postseason wrestling tournaments, weight training, and off-season sports or running.

Summer Wrestling Clinics

To improve technique, the dedicated wrestler should attend summer wrestling clinics, prepared to take notes. He should not try to learn all the moves taught during the weeklong clinic, especially those so-called clinic moves. These are maneuvers that look fancy but are rarely used or successful in competition. They are not founded on sound fundamentals. Clinicians present them to catch the eyes of the campers in order to teach the truly worthwhile moves.

The wrestler's prime objective should be to learn one or two new moves in each area of wrestling (takedowns, escapes and reversals, and rides and pinning combinations). They should be maneuvers that suit his wrestling style and body type. For example, if a wrestler is tall and thin, he should pay special attention to novel leg-wrestling moves.

Finally, the wrestler must consider the moves that he has had the most success with in past competitions. With this in mind, when the clinician demonstrates the wrestler's favorite moves, he should write down those subtle additions to the maneuver that make it even more effective in a match.

Clinics can be very worthwhile in perfecting wrestling skills if the clinic participant lives by the following two guidelines:

1. The wrestler must keep focused on the preceding suggestions.
2. The wrestler must approach the clinic as though it were a classroom. It is not to be perceived as a place for competition but as a place for learning. Therefore, he should never be afraid to ask questions!

In abiding by these guidelines, the wrestler will find the clinic experience to be of great personal benefit on the mats.

Postseason Wrestling Tournaments

Of course, there is no substitute for experience when it comes to developing wrestling skills. So if a wrestler is determined to be a state champion in today's highly competitive athletic world, he will need to compete in postseason tournaments.

On the other hand, there are some very important concerns that must be addressed regarding the advantages of postseason tournaments for the wrestler. The following are recommendations for participating in open wrestling competitions after the regular season:

1. First and foremost, the wrestler should join a well-coached wrestling club that stresses conditioning as well as the basics of the mat sport. The surest way to get seriously injured at a postseason tournament is by not being in sound physical condition. It would be a tragedy to miss in-season action due to a long-term injury sustained at a postseason wrestling tournament.

2. The wrestler should *not* be concerned with weight reduction when competing in postseason tournaments. Year-round weight watching will lead to wrestling burnout. This loss-of-desire phenomenon has ended the careers of many fine wrestlers.

3. Do not wrestle in too many postseason tournaments. Five highly competitive wrestling tournaments would suffice. You don't want to peak at the end of summer but at the end of the wrestling season . . . at the state championships!

The wrestler's goal for wrestling in postseason tournaments should be threefold: First, he should continue to use successful moves previously learned in an effort to perfect them.

Second, this is the time of the year to attempt new moves. It doesn't cost the wrestler or his school's wrestling team anything if he fails to complete a new maneuver. The key is that the wrestler learns from the experience and makes the appropriate adjustments.

Finally, the wrestler should be constantly evaluating his progress with the assistance of his club coach. Summer wrestling tournaments must be viewed as a means to an end, preparing the wrestler for competitive action during the season.

Weight Training

The three components of successful wrestling are skill development, conditioning, and strength. When opposing wrestlers are identical in skill development and conditioning, the deciding factor often becomes strength.

Weight training is a year-round endeavor if a wrestler aspires to be a state champion. Furthermore, the wrestler's priority should be to lift weights for muscle endurance strength (more reps with less weight) and not for explosive strength (fewer reps with more weight) (see chapter 8).

The wrestler's first step in initiating an off-season weight training program is to talk with his wrestling coach, strength coach, or a weightlifting trainer from the local fitness center. One of these individuals will see to it that the wrestler starts his weight training program at appropriate weights (and with the correct amount of time at each station) for his body type. Not knowing the proper weight or number of sets and repetitions to do for beginning weight training can cause serious muscular injury.

One time-tested approach is circuit training with one set of 10 repetitions for each of three weightlifting exercise cycles. The amount of weight for each exercise should be enough that the wrestler strains to accomplish the last two or three repetitions. The ideal weight training program should occur three days a week (for example, Monday, Wednesday, and Friday).

Safety is another important factor. First, it would be wise to work with a partner of similar body size so that one can spot while the other is lifting. Note also the following basic safety tips for free weights and weightlifting machines.

Free Weights

1. Take great care in putting the weights on the bar evenly; otherwise the bar could tip, potentially causing injury.
2. Make sure all weights are locked securely.
3. Be on the lookout for bars that are shoulder height or above. Athletes could get serious facial injuries by walking into the bar.
4. Put barbells, dumbbells, and weight plates away when you are finished so that nobody trips over them.

Weightlifting Machines

1. See to it that the selector keys are inserted all the way.
2. Place levers and seats at locations that suit your body size.
3. Establish a stable sitting and foot-support base when performing exercises.
4. Keep hands and fingers as far as possible from any moving objects on the weightlifting machine.

Always remember that off-season weight training is just as important to the dedicated wrestler as in-season weight training.

Off-Season Sports

A final concern for the wrestler in the off-season is to be actively involved in enhancing his cardiovascular endurance. This can be accomplished via many avenues of physical activity. We will begin with off-season sports.

In the spring, the wrestler could compete in track and field. The wrestler who is sincere about his physical endurance should compete in long-distance events, such as the 1,500- or 3,000-meter events.

Baseball is another great spring competition; it is outstanding for short sprint training but not for endurance workouts. Should a wrestler choose to play baseball, great! However, he should also consider doing extra running or swimming during the spring and summer seasons.

Two great autumn activities that are conducive to cardiovascular efficiency are cross-country and soccer. The diligent wrestler would be wise to compete in one of these two sports before wrestling season.

Finally, the most popular American sport of the fall—football—is another athletic prospect for the wrestler during the autumn months. Like baseball, this extremely physical sport also requires brief bursts of physical activity during competition, but not stamina. So the serious wrestler who plays football needs to add running to his daily routine.

Off-Season Running

If a wrestler is not competing in off-season sports that promote physical endurance, he must design his own running program (see chapter 8). Following is an off-season running plan that has worked for many champion wrestlers. It coincides with the weight training schedule described in the previous section.

Because the wrestler is lifting on Monday, Wednesday, and Friday, he should run on the alternate days—Tuesday, Thursday, and Saturday. Sunday would be a day of rest. These recommendations will maximize the effectiveness of a running program:

1. The wrestler must first perform flexibility exercises for the legs and arms before running.

2. During the summer months, the wrestler should run in the mornings and carry water to beat the heat.

3. The wrestler should run 4 to 6 miles (6-10 km).

4. Interval training is an outstanding strategy for running. This method involves alternating between running and sprinting. For example, the wrestler's initial pace could involve 7- to 9-minute miles, depending on his body build. If in doubt, he should ask for his coach's advice. While running, the wrestler would sprint 30 seconds every two minutes, timing himself with a stopwatch. Substitutes for sprinting include running up hills or steps during the workout.

5. When the wrestler's run is completed, he should cool down by walking for 10 to 15 minutes. At this time, he should also drink enough water to make him feel comfortable.

Off-season activities are important for wrestlers who want to succeed in the mat sport. Summer wrestling clinics, postseason wrestling tournaments, weight training, and off-season sports and running are prerequisites for such achievement. As their coach, you are responsible for guiding them in such a positive direction.

CONCLUSION

The key to a championship wrestling program is how well you organize your daily practice drill and workout sessions to fit the needs of your wrestlers. It is also up to you to develop and enact a well-rounded yearlong strategy your wrestlers can follow. To use a movie-production metaphor, you are the producer, the script writer, and the director—do not let the actors down!

About the Editor

William A. (Bill) Welker, EdD, boasts over 55 years of experience as a successful wrestler, coach, and official. He is a former Pennsylvania Interscholastic Athletic Association (PIAA) state champion and PIAA state runner-up. Welker also competed at the collegiate level for the University of Pittsburgh.

As head sophomore coach at Wheeling Park High School (West Virginia), he was instrumental in producing three AAA state championship teams. For his efforts as a high school coach, Welker was selected as one of the top wrestling coaches in the country by *Scholastic Wrestling News*. He has coached wrestling at the youth, middle school, and high school levels for three decades.

In 2005, Welker retired after 25 years as a wrestling referee. During his officiating tenure, he has been named the West Virginia Official of the Year (1990), the National Federation of State High School Associations (NFHS) Mideast Section Distinguished Official of the Year (2001), and the National Official of the Year by *Wrestling USA* magazine (2002).

Since 1989, Welker has been the West Virginia state clinician, rules interpreter, and state tournament supervisor of officials. He is currently serving on the NFHS national wrestling rules committee.

Welker has written over 600 articles on the art and science of wrestling since 1974. He was named the National Sportswriter of the Year by *Wrestling USA* magazine in 1987, and he has received the West Virginia Snyder-Miller Media Award an unprecedented seven times by the state coaches' association. He also wrote the script and produced the DVD titled *The Pancake Takedown Series* (2008), which is being distributed throughout the United States.

Welker has been inducted into four wrestling halls of fame, including the West Virginia chapter of the National Wrestling Hall of Fame and the Pennsylvania Wrestling Hall of Fame. He also received the prestigious Master of Wrestling Award from *Wrestling USA* magazine (2008).

Welker earned both his bachelor's and master's degrees from the University of Pittsburgh. He later acquired a doctorate in the field of education from West Virginia University. Upon his retirement from his 40-year teaching career in 2009, Welker was named Teacher of the Year by the Wheeling Area Chamber of Commerce.

Welker and his wife, Peggy, have four children and 13 grandchildren. They reside on Wheeling Island in Wheeling, West Virginia.

About the Contributors

Jim Akerly is the founder, director, and coach for the Quest School of Wrestling in Canonsburg, Pennsylvania, where he has produced many prominent youth, scholastic, and collegiate wrestlers. While wrestling for West Virginia University, Akerly became the third-winningest wrestler in school history, recording 119 victories, and was a silver medalist at the prestigious Midlands Tournament in 1986. He qualified for the NCAA Division I Championships three times and earned All-American laurels in 1987. As a coach, Akerly headed up the Pennsylvania freestyle and Greco national teams from 1989 to 1997. At the collegiate level, he coached at West Virginia University, Edinboro (Pennsylvania), Rider University (New Jersey), the University of Virginia, and American University in Washington, DC. While coaching at American University, he was selected as the Colonial Athletic Association's Wrestling Coach of the Year in 1997. Akerly resides in Canonsburg, Pennsylvania.

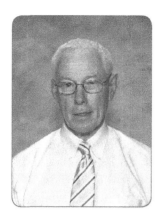

Bill Archer is the principal at St. Joseph Central Catholic High School in Huntington, West Virginia. Under his direction as head wrestling coach at Huntington High School, his teams have amassed a phenomenal dual-meet record of 426-83 (.837). Over a 33-year period at the helm, his teams have won 24 regional championships (which ranks him as one of the top 10 coaches in the state) and produced 26 individual West Virginia state champions. In 2001, the two-time state Coach of the Year was selected as the National Wrestling Coach of the Year by the National High School Coaches Association. A former West Virginia Secondary School Activities Commission (WVSSAC) state champion, Archer was the all-time winningest wrestler at Marshall University in Huntington and was inducted into the university's Athletic Hall of Fame in 2004. Archer is the state editor of *Wrestling USA* magazine and has served as the state chairman for USA Wrestling since 1986. He was selected as the 2006 West Virginia Wrestling Coach of the Year by his coaching peers and received the Master of Wrestling Award from *Wrestling USA* magazine. Archer is a member of the West Virginia chapter of the National Wrestling Hall of Fame. He holds a master's degree in educational administration. Archer and his wife, Diane, have two children and four grandchildren. They reside in Huntington, West Virginia.

Since 2001 **Bruce Burnett** has been the head coach of the Navy wrestling program with the goal of adding to the storied tradition while helping mentor what will be our nation's leaders. During his tenure, he has led the Midshipmen to a 101-50 record (.669) that featured six straight seasons of 10 or more wins from 2002 to 2007. Along the way, he has helped produce nine EIWA champions while 10 wrestlers have garnered All-American recognition under his tutelage. Burnett started his coaching career at Meridian High School in Meridian, Idaho, where he was the head coach from 1974 to 1987. In his 14 years, Burnett had a stout record of 154-13-2 (.917). His teams won nine conference, six district, and four state championships. He was named Idaho Coach of the Year six times. Burnett is a 1973 graduate of Idaho State, where he received his bachelor of arts degree in secondary education. He and his wife, Karen, live in Annapolis, Maryland.

Dave LaMotte was the head wrestling coach for the Salt River Pima-Maricopa Indian Community High School in Scottsdale, Arizona. During his 24-year coaching tenure, LaMotte has produced 17 individual state champions, 53 state place winners, 28 district titlists, and 3 high school All-Americans. LaMotte began his coaching career at his alma mater in Bridgeport, Ohio, where his 1988 team captured the Division III state championship and he was voted the Ohio Division III Coach of the Year in 1989. In 1993 LaMotte earned Coach of the Year honors when his Gilbert High School (Arizona) squad won the 5A state championship. LaMotte also coached his two sons, who were both Arizona state champions and NCAA Division II All-Americans. As a competitor, LaMotte was an all-state high school wrestler and compiled a record of 103-14-2 for West Liberty State College in West Virginia. He was also a two-time National Association of Intercollegiate Athletics (NAIA) All-American and an NAIA champion. In 2004 he was inducted into West Liberty University's Athletic Hall of Fame. LaMotte and his wife, Vickie, reside in Gold Canyon, Arizona.

Pat Pecora, who also serves as Pitt-Johnstown's athletic director since July 2008, took over the Mountain Cat wrestling program in 1976. In 36 years, his teams have captured 20 NCAA Regional Championships, including 5 straight from 2003 to 2007 and 10 in a row from 1992 through 2001. Coach Pecora has been selected as the NCAA Regional Coach of the Year 14 times. His Mountain Cat squads have finished in the top 20 in the nation 29 times and have combined to win 48 team tournaments and 500 dual meets. Coach Pecora has tutored 134 All-Americans and 10 individual national champions, including Shane Valko (133 lbs.), the 2010 National Wrestler of the Year. Academically, his teams led the nation in NWCA All-Academic wrestling team selections from 1997 through 2000. Since 1990, Coach Pecora has coached 95 NWCA All-Academic wrestling team members. In 1996 and 1999, his teams captured the NCAA Division II National Championship, the first and second in school history. In 1995 and 1999, Coach Pecora was named NCAA Division II National Coach of the Year. Also in 1999, he received the National Wrestling Coaches Association Coaching Excellence Award, given to the best coach in all divisions. Coach Pecora also coached the national all-star team, which showcased the best wrestlers in the nation from all divisions. On February 14, 2012, Coach Pecora became the first in NCAA Division II history and just the sixth in all divisions to earn 500 career dual-meet victories. He has been inducted into five halls of fame, including the Division II National Wrestling Hall of Fame and the Pennsylvania Wrestling Hall of Fame. Coach Pecora and his wife, Tracy, have four children.

The late **Edwin C. Peery** was a professor and coach emeritus for the United States Naval Academy. He was head coach of the Midshipmen wrestling team from 1960 until 1987 and retired from the Academy in 2000. During his coaching tenure, Peery posted a 311-90-14 dual-meet record, coaching eight Eastern Intercollegiate Wrestling Association (EIWA) championship teams, 48 individual EIWA titlists, and 16 NCAA All-Americans. He was named NCAA Coach of the Year in 1968 and received EIWA coaching honors in 1974 and 1986. He was an honorary lifetime member of the National Wrestling Coaches Association, having served as its president and as a member of its rules committee. A two-time Pennsylvania Interscholastic Athletic Association (PIAA) state champion, Peery won three NCAA titles under the coaching of his father, the legendary Rex Peery, at the University of Pittsburgh. Peery was also a distinguished member of the National Wrestling Hall of Fame and the Pennsylvania Wrestling Coaches Hall of Fame, and he was selected as an Outstanding American by the Maryland chapter of the National Wrestling Hall of Fame. Peery is survived by his wife, Gretchen.

Larry Shaw was the head wrestling coach at Oak Glen High School in New Cumberland, West Virginia, for 31 years, retiring in 2010. He led his Golden Bears squad on an incredible run of 13 consecutive West Virginia AA state championships from 1997 to 2009. This feat is unmatched by any other wrestling program or any other sport in West Virginia and ranks fifth among wrestling programs across the United States, tied with St. Edward's in Lakewood, Ohio. Shaw also posted five straight West Virginia AAA runner-up finishes (1987-91). He finished with a career dual-meet record of 330-96-4. Shaw coached 51 individual state champions and more than 160 others who earned all-state honors. For his efforts, Shaw was named the West Virginia AA Dix Manning Coach of the Year seven times. He is the only wrestling coach to be selected the West Virginia All-Sports Coach of the Year by the West Virginia Sports Writers Association in 2000. Shaw was also honored as the National Wrestling Coach of the Year in 2008 by *Wrestling USA* magazine. A past president of the West Virginia Wrestling Coaches Association, Shaw has promoted wrestling throughout the state and continues to do so. He has been inducted into five wrestling and sports halls of fame, including the West Virginia chapter of the National Wrestling Hall of Fame in 2010 and the NFHS National Sports Hall of Fame in 2011. Shaw and his wife, Cindy, reside in New Cumberland, West Virginia.

Ken L. Taylor has been head wrestling coach at Rocky Mountain High School in Fort Collins, Colorado, since 2001. During this time, he has led teams to 6 regional championships and 3 conference titles as well as producing 10 individual state champions. His squads have had 5 top 10 finishes at state championships. Taylor was also a 1972 NAIA All-American silver medalist for Colorado's Adams State College and captain of the school's 1972 NAIA national championship team. During Taylor's 15-year coaching tenure at Poudre High School (Colorado), his teams won four district titles and two regional championships. He also produced seven top 10 teams at the state level, six individual state titlists, and two state runner-up squads. Taylor has been voted Colorado State Wrestling Coach of the Year on three occasions. He also coached the Colorado wrestling all-star team in 1981 and 1990. Taylor and his wife, Julie, reside in Fort Collins, Colorado.

Craig Turnbull has served as the head wrestling coach at West Virginia University since 1979. He is the winningest coach in West Virginia University history, having built one of the strongest and most dominating wrestling programs in the United States. His teams have compiled a record of 265 dual-meet wins, ranking him the seventh-winningest active coach in Division I wrestling. He produced 42 Eastern Wrestling League (EWL) champions, 26 All-Americans, 7 NCAA finalists, and 3 wrestlers who won five NCAA Division I titles. Since he has won the NCAA Division I Rookie Coach of the Year award, Turnbull's squads have consistently placed in the top 25 nationally. In 1990, Turnbull was selected as the Eastern Wrestling League's Coach of the Year as West Virginia University captured its first Eastern Mat Poll No. 1 ranking. Turnbull was also selected to coach the National Wrestling Coaches Association's All-Star Classic in 1992. He has been named the EWL's Coach of the Year three times and has won five Eastern Dual Meet Championships from 1990 to 2003. Turnbull is a member of the Wesleyville-Iroquois-Lawrence Park Hall of Fame and the Metro Erie chapter of the Pennsylvania Sports Hall of Fame. He is currently a board member of the National Wrestling Coaches Association. Coach Turnbull and his wife, Sue, have two children and reside in Morgantown, West Virginia.